CHASING A CROATIAN GIRL

CHASING A CROATIAN GIRL

A SURVIVOR'S TALE

CODY McCLAIN BROWN

Chasing a Croatian Girl: A Survivor's Tale
Copyright © 2015 by Cody McClain Brown
All rights reserved.

Printed in the United States of America by CreateSpace.

No part of this book may be used or reproduced in any form without written permission of the copyright owner.

www.facebook.com/chasingacroatiangirl
www.facebook.com/Zablogreb
Twitter @smedj

ISBN-13: 978-1516959549
ISBN-10: 151695954X

Third Edition: August 2015

Book design by Walsh Branding.

Illustrations by Cody McClain Brown.

For Mara, so you'll know how and why.

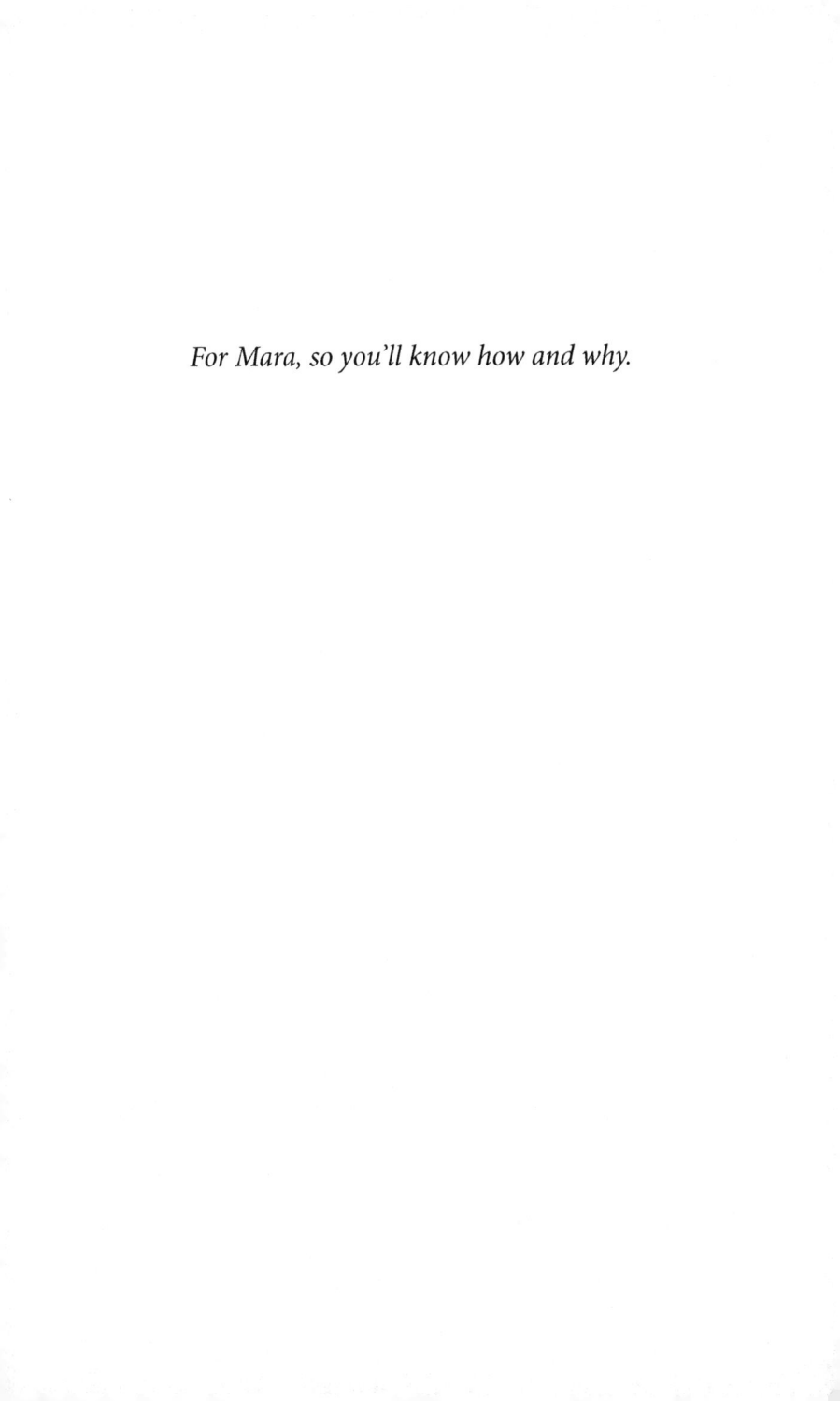

TABLE OF CONTENTS

A Note from the Author

1 *Croatia: Where Russia Isn't* 15

2 *Croatian Girls Ain't Easy* 21

SPLIT ★ PART 1

3 *Gift Giving* 34

4 *Having Coffee in Croatia* 39

5 *Lunchtime* 47

6 *Dalmatians and the Sea (with pictures)* 54

7 *Friendship* 63

8 *Family and Cramped Quarters* 68

9 *U.S.A.* 72

10 *Croatian Service, Keeping it Real, Really Real* 76

SPLIT ★ PART 2

11 *Split* 84

12 *Neighbors* 88

13 *Baby* 95

14 *The Bare Feet Cry Freedom* 102

15 *Propuh, the Murderous Wind* 108

16 *Fashion* 116

17 *The Wonderful World of Zetdom* 120

ZAGREB

18 *Zagreb* 128

19 *Finding an Apartment* 132

20 *Why My Punica is Like a Drug Dealer* 138

21 *Drinking* 144

22	*Party Breaking*	150
23	*Splitting the Ticket*	156
24	*Wild West vs. Mild East*	160
25	*Veze*	168
26	*The Dark Side*	172
27	*Lines*	176
28	*ZET*	180
29	*Zablogreb*	185
30	*Giving My Daughter the American Dream?*	189

Epilogue: Punica Goes to America 193

Acknowledgments 203

About the Author 204

A NOTE FROM THE AUTHOR

This book is based on my real life experiences, but most of the names have been changed to protect the innocent. Some of the characters have been merged into one another, some of the places have been changed, others have been made up entirely, and most of the generalizations are exaggerated and should not be taken as the incontrovertible truth.

Just go with it. Laugh with me. Or at me.

CHAPTER 1

Croatia: Where Russia Isn't

The first night I met my wife was in a small town in rural Oklahoma. She'd said she was from Croatia. I thought that meant Russia. It happened to be one of the coldest nights of the year and our evening class in comparative politics had just ended. As I, and the other grad students hurried to our cars, I watched Vana walk away into the frigid distance, back across the campus, toward the apartments where all the foreign students lived. You could tell she was from Europe—tall and svelte, she was an elegant, passing shadow. With her hands shoved in her pockets and her head down, the strands of her long hair made halos underneath the street lights. Even her steps seemed to contain a level of sophistication missing in the blundering footfalls of us Okies who were in mid-stampede to the parking lot.

Given that it was freezing, I thought that the nice, gentlemanly, thing to do would be to offer her a ride. I also worried that such an offer would send shivers all over her creepy scale. Divided between the desire to be kind, and not wanting to come off as a weirdo, I drove off, and halfway to the corner decided to go ahead and offer her a lift. I doubled-back, driving in the way I imagined she was walking, but there was no sign of her. Like a ghost she had faded into the night. As I turned toward home, I thought: Oh well, she's from Croatia. She must be used to the cold.

I couldn't have been more wrong. As it turns out, Vana is actually from Split, an ancient city on the Adriatic Sea. Not only is Split rarely freezing cold, the average temperature is 67° F, it's also one of sunniest places in Europe.

Of course I, like most Americans didn't really know where or even what Croatia was. As we can see from my example, even those of us in graduate school may need a lesson in geography. Then again, I'll also bet that most Croatians, or even Europeans cannot find Oklahoma on a map of America. So we're even. Not really. The problem with my not knowing where Croatia was, was that I didn't even know I didn't know. I was convinced I knew where Croatia was: somewhere in RUSSIA! My deficiency in geographical knowledge was coupled with an absurd confidence. Awesome! America!

Part of the blame for this ignorance is the U.S.'s own geography. We live between two, huge-ass oceans and tend to lump everything on the other side into the category of "over there." Growing up during the Cold War didn't help matters much either. The reductiveness of the bipolar political world made geography a cinch. If it was European and Communist, it was Russian, meaning anything and everything behind the Iron Curtain had abysmal winters, long lines, and sad, sad people yearning to wear Levi's and eat McDonald's. My mental map of the Cold War world was partitioned between free, colorful, bright democracies and the dark repressive spaces of the "Evil Empire." The specifics didn't matter. So when Vana told our class she was from Croatia, I figured, Croatia, Chechnya, Dagestan, Azerbaijan, Yugoslavia, Serbia, Siberia, Belarus, Armenia, Bulgaria, Ukraine, Moldova—all the same. All former Communist. All poor. All war-torn. All once part of some bigger shitty something that broke into a billion tiny shittier little somethings.

It wasn't even until I happened to be looking at an old map of the Soviet Union from a 1988 issue of *National Geographic*, a month or so later, that I: a) noticed that the socialist federation Croatia had once been a part of, Yugoslavia, wasn't even part of the Soviet Union; And b) that Croatia IS. ACROSS. FROM. ITALY! *What? Italy?* Followed by this epiphany: *Wow. It's probably not even that cold there.* (I graduated with honors ladies and gentlemen! With. Honors!) Intrigued more by my own ignorance than any real interest in Croatia, I began doing a bit of research.

A few days later I was able to put my knowledge to good use. During our evening class's 10-minute break, while Vana and a few other students were smoking, someone asked her about Croatia, Yugoslavia and Communism. In the question was the assumption that Croatia was in or part of Russia. *Hmph, morons.* Vana tried to correct this assumption. I politely offered that actually, Croatia is right next to Italy and that during the Roman Empire it was the Roman equivalent of Florida, and even the Roman Emperor Diocletian, built his "retirement" palace on the coast. Vana looked taken aback.

"Pretty much," she said.

Over the semester I started to create a cognitive map of Croatia and the rest of Southeastern Europe. I began first by imagining Italy as a boot (original, I know), and Croatia being across from the backside of the leg, just below the knee and not quite taking up the whole calf. To the immediate north of the country is Slovenia, which is like the Canada of the Balkans: Cleaner. Colder. Lamer. Then you have Croatia's Eastern neighbor, Serbia, which I imagined to be sort of like how Texas is to Oklahoma. It's bigger, a bit better known (and not in a good way), wilder, and probably a bit crazier. People know you don't mess with Texas. Below Croatia is Bosnia, and well everyone in the U.S. has at least heard of Bosnia. We know we once did something there somewhere with CNN. Then running along the western edge of Bosnia is Croatia's pristine Dalmatian

Coast, which I knew as Rome's Florida and many Americans today know as the place Rick Steves, Bill Gates and Beyoncé go and where HBO films *Game of Thrones*. Below the coast is Montenegro. That's all I know about Montenegro.

Again, to be fair to my American compatriots, it is hard for most of us to understand the dynamics of national change that once afflicted all of Europe and still afflicts parts of Southeastern Europe. The United States has what many countries are lacking: continuity. With the exception of the Civil War, we have been one country since the late 18th century. Since coming over on the boat, all of my family members have been born all over America, but all IN America. Whereas my Croatian daughter, wife, mother-in-law, and her mother, great-grandma Julia, have all been born in the same place, but each in a DIFFERENT country. What? Seriously? Yes. Crazy! I know!

America is like Coke. It's the brand everyone knows. Since 1776 the United States of America has been the United States of America. While there has been ample growth in the U.S.'s market share, it has, for over 200 years been branded America (apologies to Canada and Mexico). Croatia in that same amount of time has had issues with its name recognition and maintaining its brand identity.[1] Growing up in the U.S. we just take our country's stability and longevity for granted. It's hard for us to understand or even comprehend that the lines

---

1 See page 20.

on maps may have little meaning to much of the world, or that states rise and fall. We assume away the complexities of the world with a binary vision based on our own experience. Things are either here or there, us or them, normal or...Eur-O-pean. The more I learned about Croatia and the closer I grew to Vana, the weaker this diametric world view became. I began to see the world in more vibrant colors than the mundane gray I had assumed gathered on the edges of America.

As the semester drew to a close, I was looking forward to us spending the summer together in this small, desolate, Oklahoma town. Then she announced that she was moving to New York for the summer. *Shit.*

---

1 In the last 200 or so years Croatia has been: The Republic of Croatia and the 28th member of the European Union, the Socialist Republic of Croatia in the Socialist Federal Republic of Yugoslavia, The Independent State of Croatia, Yugoslavia: The Kingdom of Serbs, Croats and Slovenes, The Kingdom and Lands Represented in the Imperial Council and the Lands of the Holy Hungarian Crown of Saint Stephen (better known as The Austrian-Hungarian Empire), and parts of Croatia were all simultaneously parts of The Austrian Empire, The Habsburg Empire, The Ottoman Empire, The Venetian Republic, and The Kingdom of Hungary. Dang!

CHAPTER 2

Croatian Girls Ain't Easy

"Hmm," Vana muttered, rather unimpressed. We were in the New York Metropolitan Museum of Art, standing in a reconstructed ancient Egyptian temple, and all she could say was, "Hmm?"

My eyes widened, and then narrowed in disappointment. Maybe I was all wrong about this girl. Who can stand before a piece of ancient history and look at it with casual indifference? Then she went on.

"This reminds me of my town. It's just like this," she said, and then put her hands against the walls of the narrow, stone hallway. "There's a street just like this, called *pusti me da prodjem*, please let me pass." She turned looking at the stones again, nodded and said: "Yep, just like this," before walking on.

I was dumbfounded. Her town has stone walls like ancient Egypt? I mean weren't most of the towns in Eastern Europe comprised of huge socialist housing blocks that make our housing projects look quaint? Ancient stuff? Huh? I hurried after her, confused. I was of course still embarrassingly ignorant of Croatia. Even though I had read up a little bit and become more precise in my geography, I still maintained a mental image of Vana's homeland as one of snow, socialism, statues of dictators, and scarved peasant women walking around with bundles of sticks strapped to their backs. My mental picture of Croatia was something between a Soviet-style military parade and the whimsy of a Chagall painting.

That trip to New York was plagued with cultural misunderstandings. What I took to be Vana's romantic interest in me, turned out to be little more than great examples of Croatian hospitality.

In the waning days of the semester, Vana and I kept running into each other. Granted, in a small town with only two semi-decent bars, this is not all that difficult; however, at the time, I imagined these chance meetings to be some kind of cosmic coincidence turned by the gears of fate, forcing us to interact. We talked about politics, nationalism, George W. Bush, terrorism, New Order, the War, TBF, Bijelo Dugme, Hermann Hesse, the Warriors, Hair, Deep Purple, Kraftwerk and a myriad of other things, few, if anyone in ultraconservative Oklahoma shared my views about. I felt there was something between us, something deeper and bigger than ourselves, something that carried the weight of an unseen, but in some way inevitable future. Fate, I guess. In our own way we were both unique to the landscape surrounding us. I was probably just as much an outsider as she was, an exotic specimen in a small, redneck town.

Before attending graduate school in Oklahoma I had left the state, hoping to never return. I went to school in New Orleans for three years, and lived in Montreal for one. I had held the aspirations to become a world traveler and a great writer. In my spare time I tried to prepare for my expat, writerly existence by reading books by Noam Chomsky, Solzhenitsyn, Robert Fisk, Thomas Pynchon, Albert Camus, Marx and Lenin. Yet, instead of going global, I ended up back in Oklahoma working at a large chain bookstore. Then I got in a physical altercation with another employee, in the middle of the store, in front of a customer. There were complaints. There was an inquiry. There was me being fired (the other guy got fired too).

I threw one punch, and that punch happened to be the best, dumbest thing I have ever done in my entire life. Of course, I didn't see it like that at the time. After getting fired for a half-second of rash impulse, I thought that my life was over. Little did I know, it was just the beginning. Everything I am today, everything I am involved in, began when I got fired from the bookstore. If I hadn't punched that guy I would probably still be working there today.

After getting fired I painted houses with my dad. This was the job I had held during my teenage summers when all I could do was dream about leaving Oklahoma. Now, here I was 24, right back where I started, as if my life in Montreal and New Orleans had never happened. Painting houses was also a lonely job. It was usually just me, the brush, the paint and the wall. I needed work with more social interaction, with some sort of greater purpose behind it. I decided to go to the State University to try and use my Bachelor's degree to become a high school English teacher. Through a series of odd circumstances I ended up enrolling in a Master's in Political Science, and the next semester I met Vana on that cold winter's night. Now, at the end of that semester, Vana seemed like everything I had so far failed to be.

She was smart, exciting, and beautiful. She had already lived a life with more meaning and interest than mine. She had lived through the breakup of a country, a war, and even reported on events in the war. And here she was now, studying abroad. I was envious. Talking with her opened me up to new perspectives that the old binary thinking had a difficult time computing. My time with her was both challenging and enlightening.

I also loved her little cultural idiosyncrasies. Whenever she was outside smoking at her apartment she put the town's thin phone book on the ground and sat on it. When I was there she offered me the extra phone book. (Much later, I would find out this phone book thing was a consequence of the Croatian belief that her ovaries would freeze if she sat directly on the concrete, and her being a foreign student, she didn't have anything else to sit on outside. Since I don't have ovaries, I still have no idea why she offered me one). She always insisted on paying for everything. In her mid-30s, she still stayed up until dawn and slept until 2 p.m. And her English was hypnotic. Each word was chosen with a cautious, careful deliberation and so wonderful to listen to that you just wanted to lay next to her and hear her talk until you died.

She also confused the shit out of me. She was like an enigma, wrapped in a riddle, swaddled in cigarette smoke with an accent. In all the time we spent with each other, nothing happened. One time she grabbed my hand after we lost each other in a bar, but that was the extent of our physical involvement. I thought she was at least giving me some romantic cues, but it never seemed like the right time, and I never had enough nerve to push it. I didn't understand what was happening or if we were trying to be more than friends.

Men in the U.S. have the misconception that girls from any post-Communist country are easy and are willing to sleep with us just because we are Americans. We are under the impression that wherever anyone lives in Central or Eastern Europe, it must be so awful and depressing that any girl would jump at the chance to be with an American. Again, this probably goes back to the Cold War, when we were told that everyone living under Communism was miserable and willing to do ANYTHING to escape the misery of the Workers' Paradise. Rumors abound about how Czech or Polish girls would sleep with you for a pack of authentic Marlboros, Levi's jeans, or hard currency. Even in the post-Cold War world, many of us remain under this impression. Instead of rescuing women from behind the Iron Curtain, we are now under the delusion that we can save them from a life of poverty and political corruption. We have stories of mail-order brides and other fantasy-laden legends. We see ourselves as romantic liberators ready to help beautiful women date their way to freedom. It's ridiculous. We imagine life in East Europe as a Hobbesian nightmare: short, brutish, and nasty. At the same time, we imagine all the young women to be tall, hot, and sexy!

A great example of this fantasy even comes from shows with such tepid sex humor as *The Big Bang Theory*. In one episode, one of the nerds is online saying that there are "hundreds of Croatian girls waiting for you to contact them at anythingforagreencard.com." Well, guess what guys, few Croatians are willing to do much, less anything for a green card. Most Croatians I've met would like to VISIT America, few, if any would like to LIVE here. If they do, it's because they haven't been. Those that go, come running back, if they can. Those that can't come back, dream of one day being able to return.

Croatia is a beautiful country with what might be the world's most beautiful coastline. Not to mention a wonderful and rich way of life that makes life in Oklahoma look Hobbesian. Who would give up the Adriatic Sea and their home, to live in some landlocked state like Oklahoma, Missouri, or Kansas? Few. That's who.

While Vana did not show much inclination to being intimate with me, she kept doing things that indicated some level of romantic interest. Looking back years later, I see she was just being Croatian.

NEW YORK CULTURAL MISUNDERSTANDING #1: When she told me she was moving to New York for the summer, she of course invited me to visit her. I took this to mean she must like me. I was unaware that Croatians are very hospitable and out of politeness invite everyone everywhere, especially if they sense that you would like them to say you can come visit them. Out of politeness, they will tell you to visit. I've been politely invited to stay on the island Vis about 10 billion times and have never taken anyone up on their offer. Most invitations exist in that special space between politeness and sincerity. In Croatia, it's normal when talking about going somewhere to someone that you mention they should come visit you. It definitely doesn't mean this girl is into you.

NEW YORK CULTURAL MISUNDERSTANDING #2: A month or so later, I booked a ticket first to D.C. and took a bus to New York. When Vana met me she had gifts for me. Three books to be precise. I took this as the second sign that she must be into me. Nope. In Croatia people give gifts to everyone for every possible reason, and more commonly for no reason at all. Really. They're gift-giving fools. Gifts definitely do not mean a girl is into you.

In any case, these misunderstood cultural cues put us on a collision course for what is probably the most awkward situation anyone can ever have. Imagine that scene at the end of the first date where you've walked her to her door. There is a pause and in the interval of a heartbeat the evening's electric tension surges for a kinetic release. A kiss! You lean in, your lips yearning for the soft press of tender skin. A warm reply to your nervous query. But, instead all you find is empty air. The next thing you know, you're getting a handshake and a voice talking about what a nice time it was. Now imagine a scene like that, but replace her front door with a friend's borrowed bed, and the expectations of a kiss with something loftier. Yep. I'm even embarrassed writing about it. Through a series of manipulations of time and space, late-night hours, Metro stops and bus schedules, I disastrously engineered it so that Vana and I would have to sleep together in the same bed.

The next morning we woke up in my friend's borrowed bedroom in Brooklyn. She lay stretched out beside me, the sheets were tangled between us, and we were in the awkward morass of now knowing that I had *much* stronger feelings for her than she for me. In the wee hours of the morning, buzzing with beer and exhaustion, I had tried to move this friendship to the next level. Tried and failed. At that time there was no other level. The elevator stopped in the lobby, the escalator was broken, and the stairs were out of order.

Surprisingly, I didn't feel that abashed. Instead, I felt relieved, even brimming with a new form of confidence. My desperate, disastrous plan had floundered. It would clearly take more to establish a romantic relationship with this woman…CHALLENGE ACCEPTED!

Even in the aftermath of such an embarrassing evening, I continued to feel the weight of something massive between us. Something nearly celestial, and I believe the gravity of that fate-bound mass was able to warp the situation, like a lens bends light, in such a way that we were able to finally see each other clearly. In that little Brooklyn bedroom, on the heels of our awkward evening, I believe Vana really saw me for the first time.

"Listen," I said. "I'm supposed to leave tomorrow, but if you don't want to see me tonight, I can leave today." Sitting up in the bed, she studied me askance. I think she was a bit surprised that after all this, I still wanted to see her. Then she said the most Croatian thing any Croatian can ever say. The Croatian answer to everything:

"Let's have coffee." She replied.

"Now? Or tonight?"

"Now." And so we got up, dressed and went across the street to have coffee.

I picked her up from her work at 7 p.m. in midtown Manhattan. We walked south, through Soho and into Little Italy and then Chinatown. We ate, drank, and talked. With an assuredness that I'm sure bordered between arrogance and self-delusion, I explained to Vana what I KNEW would happen.

"I'm going to leave, and you are going to miss me. Then your friends will come and visit you, and you'll miss me. You'll go back to Croatia and miss me. And so this whole time you're going to be thinking about me, missing me. And then when you come back to Oklahoma, I'll be there and you'll be there. And it will happen."

Like any sane person she seemed skeptical. We passed by the fish markets and Chinese restaurants. At a nearby bar we met up with some of my friends and had one last drink together. When she finished we knew it was time to say goodbye. Outside, the sidewalk was bustling with people. In the near distance the Empire State Building towered into a night sky punctuated by a full moon. I wanted to kiss her. I think we hugged. Then, smiling she began walking to the subway.

"Think of me!" I jokingly hollered from the steps up to the bar. She turned back with open arms and yelled:

"How can I not?" And with that she was gone, engulfed by the crowd.

SPLIT ★ PART 1

CHAPTER 3

Gift Giving

A year and a half after the events in New York, Vana and I traveled together to Croatia. It was my first time to visit. Contextually speaking, it was my first time to visit the woman I loved's homeland, the first time meeting her family, the first time to be with her in her most natural surroundings. But, more than that, I was jazzed about traveling to a former Communist country, a land once ravaged by war, a place whose name I grew up with in the noise of the evening news and NPR. I planned on excitement!

So, what did I do to prepare for this sojourn? Get some shots? Pack extensively? Bring a knife? Make sure we had all of our prescribed medications? Nope. None of that. Before you go to Croatia you need to focus on the important stuff, spending hours, days shopping for gifts.

The week before leaving we spent HOURS and DAYS, looking for gifts for almost everyone Vana knew, which as far as I was concerned, was close to nearly everyone in Croatia. We finally bought a picture for person A, a necklace for person B, sweets for person C, alcohol for person D and so on. Even at the airport Vana was scouring the overpriced souvenir shops looking for last-minute gifts.

If you haven't guessed already, gift giving is a big deal in Croatia (remember how all of one chapter ago, she gave me three books in New York for no apparent reason). In Croatia it goes like this: come back from a trip: bring gifts. Go to dinner at someone's house: bring gifts! See someone you haven't seen in a while: bring a gift. Just look at someone: give her a gift! See the doctor, minister, principal, mechanic, bus driver: gift, gift, gift, gift, gift.

As the plane took off, I was beyond excited to be heading to Vana's homeland, happily anticipating a warm Slavic reception (I had seen movies) as we distributed all of those carefully selected gifts.

Ha-ha. You know what's a little funny? OK, actually A LOT of funny, is that for all the emphasis on gift giving, most gifts are never ever even used! (Especially not by their original recipient.) In most Croatian houses there is a closet or a cupboard, sometimes just a drawer, and in the deep dark recesses of that secret space is...a pile of...RECYCLED PRESENTS! Yes! Re-gifting is as much a part of gift giving, as um...the gift giving. And once a gift is given, I would later learn, it finds itself condemned to the mysterious gift vortex (which is like limbo for gifts). It will never be opened, eaten, or drank. Instead it will swirl around in the void, passing from one giver to another, then to another and so on. Since you might always need to give someone a gift at any moment of the day, you always need to have several gifts on hand. Therefore most gifts end up in the secret gift closet and are then given again as gifts. Few if all of the carefully selected gifts we had bought were ever going to be used by their initial recipients. Of course, I didn't know this.

In the days after we arrived we distributed the gifts. A few months later on our next visit, I was confused when I saw that the gift we gave to person A, in this case the picture, somehow ended up on the wall of person C's house. Or the necklace we bought for person B, ended up on the neck of person D's daughter-in-law! Wha? Huh?

Gift giving in Croatia is like some altruistic circle of life. Fittingly for Europe, it's like a roundabout you can't quite exit from, while in America we give gifts like we are on a one-way street, mostly on your birthday and at Christmas. And in my family we even draw names so we only have to buy a gift for one person. And we put a money limit on it. That's right. During the season of giving we give as little as possible to one person.

If you return from a trip you can bring gifts back for your relatives' kids, but still. Buying gifts for your sister, nieces, nephews, cousins, uncles, aunts, in-laws, godparents, neighbors, friends, and the occasional, casual acquaintance is, believe it or not, very uncommon. My uncle ONCE brought me back a gift from Florida. And that was a bust, it was a prepackaged seashell collection, or to a six-year-old kid, the equivalent of socks on Christmas. I'd been hoping for He-Man.

After this initial trip to Croatia, when we began living between these two worlds, Vana would insist I take presents back to EVERYONE each time I returned to the States. It was awful. Want to make a situation awkward in America, give an unexpected gift. We don't know how to accept it. We think: *what the? should we eat it now? drink it? WHAT DO WE DO? And smiiiiiiiile.*

Want to make it extremely awkward, give a gift from abroad to a person you only talk to when their trash-can lids blow over into your yard. If I showed up at my neighbor's house in America with a gift from Croatia, I imagine this older gentleman would just scratch himself, look suspiciously at the parcel in my hand, squint at the unintelligible foreign words written across the top of it and yell: "Huh? You went where? What the hell is a Croatia?"

On the flight, I really still didn't know what the hell a Croatia was either. We flew from Istanbul in a prop plane to Sarajevo, my mind reeling with various imagined scenes and manifestations of what I would find there.[2] Something still like Chagall and Stalin. There was also something certainly romantic (and a little terrifying) about flying with the woman you love amid the drone of twin propellers carrying you high over the Balkans and into a snow-laden Sarajevo. I felt Bogart-esque, as if we were the stars in our own old black and white movie.

From Sarajevo we took a bus to Split. Even coming into town in the dead of night, the streets vacant, the shops shuttered, and shadows of trash-like sleeping lumps under the yellow lamplight, couldn't detract from the city's beauty. From the bus station I looked out over the harbor, awed by the boats moored along the quay and St. Duje's tower rising in the distance.

Upon stepping into Split, I felt a calmness I had never known in my life as a minor vagabond. Istanbul, New Orleans, and Montreal had always felt foreign to me. Split, immediately felt like home. At the same time, I felt an exhilarating kind of energy. Maybe it was the radiance of Vana's excitement to be home. Or it just might have been the relief of getting off of the bus after eight hours of driving in the mountains. Whatever it was, it felt good to finally be in Croatia.

---

[2] Did I mention that we were living together in Istanbul at the time? No? Oh, well we were living together in Istanbul at the time, in a Kurdish ghetto called Tarlabaşi, filled with Kurds, Roma, African immigrants and transvestites. Really. But, all I can say about Istanbul is, it's nice. You should go there. You'll like it. And if you think I really found Croatia more enticing and exciting than Istanbul, well the truth is I DID. I was more exhilarated to be flying to Croatia, via Bosnia, than I was about getting to see the GODDAMN PYRAMIDS. That's a fact. Oh right, I was also in Egypt the summer before all this too.

CHAPTER 4

Having Coffee in Croatia

The next morning we went for coffee. When Vana suggested that we go for coffee, it sounded like a great idea. I was already captivated by Split, just from what I had seen on the bus ride into town. I was eager to grab a Starbucks and walk around the town, fueling my sightseeing with a steady supply of warm caffeine.

Now I realize there were so, so many, many, many things wrong with these assumptions.

First, at the time of writing Croatia doesn't even have a Starbucks. While there are Starbucks across the street from each other in America, three on the same street in Istanbul, locations in the Czech Republic, Poland, Bulgaria, and Romania, Croatia doesn't have a single one. Oh, there were plans to build one in Zagreb, but these were delayed, indefinitely. And when you consider how much Croatians love drinking coffee, this is particularly strange.

Even before arriving in Croatia I knew Croatians loved drinking coffee. Here are some empirics. According to a 2009 survey, Croatians annually drink 5 kg of coffee per person, that's 22,500 tons of coffee per year! And they spend 2.25 million hours having coffee each year, that's half an hour a day, per person. And this doesn't mean coffee at home, this means drinking coffee out. There are so many cafes in Croatia that if you just randomly threw a rock in any direction there is a 97% chance that if it hits anything at all, it will hit a cafe. Ninety-seven percent! Zagreb alone has over 1,000 cafes.

Croatians love coffee, but more than that, coffee in Croatia is where everything gets done. It's where friends meet, where deals are made, it's how favors are asked, it's how people are hired, fired, introduced, married, divorced, everything! Remember, it's what Vana suggested we do after we didn't do it the night before. Had we done it, we still would have had coffee. Having coffee is nearly the answer to every situation in Croatia. Everything involves coffee. Even when it doesn't. Invited to someone's house for dinner? Bring coffee!!!

BUT, having coffee in Croatia is very different than in the U.S. As you might have guessed, coffee in Croatia is a social function. In the U.S., coffee is less about being social than it is about having a boost to work harder.

Let's look at some examples.

THIS IS YOUR TYPICAL CAFE IN THE HEART OF SPLIT.

Notice most of the tables are occupied by more than one person and they all look like they are talking to each other (there is one guy sitting alone, and he's wearing a shirt with an American flag! That will make sense in a minute.) People are not just sitting and playing with their smartphones, but talking, conversing, sharing in the company of friends, hangin'.

NOW LET US TURN TO A PICTURE OF YOUR TYPICAL AMERICAN STARBUCKS.

Please notice that everyone, E-V-E-R-Y-ONE is A-LONE. Don't let that illusionary couple in the back fool you. If you look closely you'll see he is just sitting at a different table in front of her, and she is typing on a laptop. No one is talking. They're all probably listening to their iPods. And they all seem engaged in some kind of work. Saying you are going to work while having coffee to a Croatian is like saying *I'm going to put a bunch of vinegar in my milk and drink it.* You. Just. Don't. Do. It. Croatians are like: you don't go have coffee to work! You go to talk, meet, relax a little, but not to sit and listen to Arcade Fire on your "earbuds" while cramming for the final exam for your course "Intro to the Formless Forms of Postmodernism." In Croatia that's what libraries are for, duh!?!

Coffee for Americans is about the same as gasoline for cars. We drink it so we can get going and keep going. Just look at the amounts it comes in: 12, 16, 20, 31 ounces (354 ml, 473 ml, .59 and .91 liters! Almost a liter of coffee!). We also like to put lids on our coffee so we can go back to work, walk or jog while drinking our coffee. (Jog while drinking coffee? Yes.) Another reason for the varying sizes is that they serve as a status symbol (somewhat akin to the black BMW in Croatia). The bigger the cup, the more important you are. YOU ARE SO IMPORTANT YOU HAVE ONEBILLIONTHINGSTODO AND YOUCANONLY DOTHISBYDRINKINGALLOFTHISCOFFEE!!! AAAARGH!!! When I was in grad school, I thought a good way to set myself apart from the undergrads was to order the biggest coffee I could find and then shove a huge stack of thick books under my arm and walk around the campus with an air of rushed importance.

HERE ARE SOME EXAMPLES OF STARBUCKS' COFFEE SIZES:

Now I will show you the largest cup of coffee in Croatia.

Ready.

No peeking.

BEHOLD!

No. Really. This really is the biggest size you can get… ANYWHERE!

Back in Split we ran into a few of Vana's friends and had coffee together. OK, so we weren't going to walk around and drink coffee and there was no Starbucks, but at least I was going to drink coffee. I just ordered what Vana ordered *Kavu sa šlagom*, coffee with whipped cream.

IT SOUNDED SOMETHING LIKE THIS:

INSTEAD I GOT THIS:

I felt like Crocodile Dundee when he shows that punk kid a real knife. In my head I was all like: That's not a cup of coffee. This is a cup of coffee. And it was going to get worse. In the hands of a Croatian that little cup of coffee is magic. It actually holds more coffee than it appears to. Not really, it has a very, very, very small amount of coffee in it. But with a Croatian drinking, that little cup is nearly endless. A Croatian can make a single coffee last for two maybe three hours. Three. Hours. On. A. Single. Tiny. Cup. Of. Coffee.

So there I was, served this tiny, Lilliputian-sized coffee that I drank in, oh say, five minutes (probably more like two). Then I looked around and saw everybody else had full cups and I thought: Oh boy, we are going to be here awhile. And we were. Coffee in Croatia is less about that coffee and more about socializing. I sat there and everybody talked, talked, talked. By the time it was over I was so tired I needed…another…YEP…coffee!

Years later, I realize now that having coffee in Croatia is one of those things that sets the country apart from everywhere else I've ever lived. It's also one of the most enjoyable aspects of living here. Not just having coffee yourself, but seeing people having coffee is even a pleasure. On a January evening in Zagreb, the winter gloom is only illuminated by the bright lights of the city's innumerable cafes. You pass them in the cold, but inside you see they are warm, inviting, filled with life, men and women, young and old, gathered two to four to a table talking, laughing; you feel that the city is alive, and walking past each bright cafe you long to be a part of it. And this feeling stays with you, tugging at you, tempting to pull you into the nearest cafe. Until finally a friend calls you and says: *Idemo na kavu*. And like it was the greatest thing in the world, you say: *Da*.

CHAPTER 5

Lunchtime

My first full day in Split, Vana's mom, my future mother-in-law, cooked a large meal for lunch. Now, having a big lunch on the first day of our visit seemed intuitive, and very easily something that we would likely do in the U.S. I took it as a nice way for Vana's mom, Vida, to get to greet me and celebrate the return of her Prodigal Daughter. Having her cook a big lunch the next day, the day after that, after that, the next day, and all the other days we were there, plus a packed lunch cooked around 6 a.m., for us to eat on the airplane when we left, was not very likely to happen in America. Ever.

Each lunch contained soup, a salad, two side dishes and a main meal. Baked fish and sliced potatoes along with fish soup, all slathered in olive oil, maybe pan-fried pork chops, with a sliced cabbage salad, and baked eggplant, or chicken, with chicken soup and a carrot and beet salad, and lots and lots of something called *blitva*.

Everything every day was organized by Vida around what time we were going to eat lunch. And that lunch was of course cooked for us by Vida. She was possessed with a drive that we eat and obsessed with how much we ate, never nearly enough apparently. I was beginning to understand that this apron-clad, wooden-spoon-totting septuagenarian was the stubborn rock of the family. What I failed to understand was why this woman, born amid the carnage of the Second World War, a survivor of said war, raised in the authoritarian world of Communist Yugoslavia, who managed to make do amid the country's economic collapse in the 1980s, and then survived the 1990s War in Croatia, seemed most concerned with how much I ate every day. I mean my own mother hadn't asked me about what I was eating or had eaten since I was nine years old. Yet, my daily caloric intake would be a frequent point of contention in Croatia. I felt like food and my eating habits were how Vida received and transmitted her feelings. If I ate everything she would be in a good mood. If she was in a good mood already, then I didn't have to eat everything. As a result of the language barrier, I had no way of knowing what she really felt about me. And as I was ignorant of the cultural cues we normally rely on to understand someone, I had no sense of how all of this was going. What did she think about my relationship with Vana? Did she like me? Was she annoyed that her daughter brought home an American? Did she wish I was Dalmatian? Italian?

Was she skeptical about us? Was she worried that we would run off to the U.S. together? Did she think I was a spy? A CIA agent?[3] I had no idea.

I knew only four "polite" phrases in Croatian (*I love you, good night, my head hurts,* and *you are crazy*) and she knew very little English. The one interaction we did have without translation did little to clarify our relationship. As I was leaving the living room for some reason I muttered to Vana: *Ti si luda (you are crazy).* Then, while cleaning the floor in the bathroom, a dustpan clutched in one hand and the other gripping the broom, Vida asked in slow accented English: *Who. is. Crazee?*

Confused by the sudden use of English, I replied: *um...Vana.* This was followed by a long pause, as if she were seriously considering, weighing the veracity of my statement. Then she replied with a simple: *Yes.*

Huh? Dear reader, this is where I look at you and shrug. I had no idea what to make of that.

Vida split most of her time between having coffee and a cigarette on the balcony, to being engulfed in a cloud of steam rising from the stove, stirring the garlic, pasta or olive oil into each pot. She ruled her home with a heavy hand of hospitality. Like a matriarchal dictator, she was the hard-headed heart of the family. If she couldn't prevent her daughter from traipsing

---

[3] The answer to that last question is yes, she did. She is still not really convinced otherwise.

around the globe and returning with some strange American, she was going to make damn sure we ate a good lunch. Lunchtime was and is non-negotiable.

You might have guessed that in Croatia, lunch is the most important meal of the day. PERIOD. If you don't eat a good lunch there is a strong likelihood you will starve and die. If you try to argue this, if you dare to suggest that you would just like a small sandwich then you will get an eyeful of scorn and maybe even a smack on the hand with a big wooden spoon.

During those first days in Croatia I became distraught about lunch's repressiveness. For years…err my entire life! I was used to eating chips and a small sandwich for lunch. All through elementary school and high school I brought my lunch: a salami sandwich (on a piece of what Croats would call "toast," no cheese, only mustard), a bag of chips, a dessert of some kind and a fruit drink. In my adult life, lunch morphed into a coffee, a cigarette, and maybe a rapidly devoured granola bar (you know, to stay healthy).

Having the day dictated by lunch and then eating a massive meal in the afternoon was a big adjustment. As it was also one of the things lowest on **MY LIST OF POSSIBLE PROBLEMS WITH GOING TO CROATIA:** *Lunchtime? Really?*

It was like living in Superman's Bizarr-o world where everything is reversed. I mean Croatians eat sandwiches for breakfast. Yes! Sandwiches for BREAKFAST! Little did I know, but dinner was very important to my American mentality. Dinner marked the end of the afternoon and the beginning of the evening, it was like twilight's happy little threshold. Without it I was lost, literally sort of meandering in the dark, uncertain of what to do with myself. Being freed from the shackles of dinnertime was a surprisingly unsettling experience. I imagine for Croatians who go to America having to suddenly organize your social life around dinnertime is an equally constraining experience. You probably want to have coffee and everyone else wants to eat.[4]

After our hours-long coffee we headed back to the apartment. Walking through the slate gray alleys in Diocletian's Palace and up the winding streets, I noticed that the city seemed deserted. And then through the passing windows we could hear the cluttered preparations for lunch, like an orchestra tuning. The clatter of cutlery, pots boiling, and plates being laid out set the stage.

---

[4] I would later learn that lunch vs. dinnertime also explains why Americans and Croatians have completely different ideas about the length of the afternoon, evening and night. In America the evening is 5–7 p.m. Anything after 7 p.m. happens at night. While in Croatia the afternoon lasts until 9 or even 10 p.m. and the evening can last…well…until morning really. (Apparently it's ALL evening until the fun stops.)

As we ascended the stairs of Vana's apartment, I encountered the varied scents of freshly cooked meals gathering on the landing of each floor. It was a comforting smell, one of ritual, care and concern. I knew that behind each door people were sitting down together or that a grandma was cooking lunch for her grandkids. It was pleasant as the smells mixed in the stairwell into one mighty smorgasbord. I had never experienced anything similar in the U.S. To me the smell of lunchtime became the smell of Croatia.

On the morning we left, Vida woke up early to cook us lunch. I was also up, packing our luggage. I had the suitcase open on the couch and was folding our clothes inside when she came in and handed me a package wrapped in plastic bags. I started to open it and she just shook her head no and pointed to the suitcase. *O-Kay*, I thought, remembering when at the airport they ask you if anyone has given you a package or anything to transport. I nodded slowly and placed it in the suitcase next to Vana's shoes. Then Vida returned with another similar package. Again I put it in the suitcase. Then another, and another, and another. Since we couldn't communicate, I had no idea what she was giving me. But, I knew better than to refuse this woman's random foodstuffs, so it all went in (Once back in Istanbul I would unpack and see that we had transported *pršut, blitva,* homemade cookies,

Cedevita (Croatian Tang), wafer cookies, and a few varieties of cheese.) With each package I sensed a sadness in Vida. She was clearly upset that her daughter was leaving.

Our language barrier was just an expression of the tension that existed between us. I felt there was some resentment that I, a foreigner, an American no less, had whisked her daughter off to Istanbul of all places, immediately after she had already lived in the U.S. for two years. Vana was again living out of the country, away from home, and clearly I was to blame. I was a foreign source of disruption to the family, like a virus or a cancer in the body.

When Vana finally got up, we were all in the kitchen having coffee. Standing over her daughter, Vida looked at me and said to her: *"See how he gets up and prepares everything early. It's good he doesn't wait until the last minute."* Pause: *"Like you."* (Ah, parents.) And that was the biggest compliment she ever gave me, but it was enough. My entire time in Split had been an evaluation, and only then did Vida know what she thought about me. The tension eased. This was a woman who was cooking at the crack of dawn in order to make sure her daughter had something good to eat on an airplane. A woman who was sending kilos of food with us as if there wasn't food in Istanbul. Clearly, her highest priority was the well-being of her daughter. And now she saw that even though I was a foreigner, an American no less, I was also someone who would take care of her daughter too. I had passed the test.

CHAPTER 6

Dalmatians and the Sea
(with pictures)

Over the next year we traveled back and forth from Istanbul to Split. We substituted the Bosnian airline and bus route -Sarajevo-Mostar-Imotski-Split- with Yugoslavia's old airline, flying from 'stanbul to Belgrade, where we usually had to spend the night, and then taking a train from Belgrade to Zagreb and a bus from Zagreb to Split (I later learned we did all of that to save just $50!). Then we did the whole thing in reverse order. On each return, as we passed through Novi Zagreb, or stood around the train station amid Zagreb's leaden winter gray, I longed to stay in Croatia. I'd stare at the large housing blocks and imagine how wonderful it would be if just one of those little lights among the amber multitudes was ours. Then we wouldn't have to wait for the train, pass through Serbia and fly on to Istanbul, where no matter how long I stayed, I unfailingly felt like a foreigner. I knew that if we had an apartment in Zagreb or in Split we could make it a home. Each time we boarded the train back east, I felt like I was holding my breath and taking another plunge into some dark turbulent water. I felt I would only breathe easier once we were back in Croatia.

In the meantime, I asked Vana to marry me, she said yes. And in the following summer we left Istanbul for good. Now most people would be ecstatic about spending a summer on the Dalmatian Coast, for nearly free. The billion-dollar tourist industry sort of supports this assumption. So wasn't I excited to spend the summer by the sea with the woman I loved? Err… sort of. For all that earlier talk about breathing and jumping into water being easier in Croatia, well, let's just say that summer I was again holding my breath and jumping, both as a metaphor for getting married and being assimilated into a Croatian family, and also in a very real way that involved me having to swim in the sea. I learned that one of the fundamental differences between Vana and me, is her love of the sea and my hostility/indifference to it. We are from two different worlds like Aquaman, but with Aquaman as a woman and me being um…not Aquaman. Or better yet, that summer felt like we were re-enacting *The Little Mermaid*, but in reverse. I was the sailor, she was Ariel, and I was expected to live under the sea (without even a musical crustacean).

The first few times we went swimming, Vana would wade into the water and then swim out into the far distance, beckoning me to come with her. I would stubbornly refuse, shaking my head like, *no-no, I'm good right here.* Then I would splash around in the shallow parts before getting bored and return to sit under the umbrella with my book. She would come back confused, and say something like:

And then she would say:

The sea is such a part of Dalmatia, that yes, for Dalmatians the idea of drowning doesn't even exist. If they have a list of bad things that can happen to you in the sea, that list is: A) very, very short; and B) drowning isn't even on it. I guess when you've grown up as one Poseidon's children, spending most of your free time swimming in the sea, and so too has everyone you've ever known, it does seem unimaginable that someone could actually drown.

BUT, let's ALL just remember that I'm from Oklahoma. That's OKLA-LANDLOCKED-MIDDLEOFMERICA-HOMA. The nearest bit of salty water is nine hours away (and in Texas, BLECH). Needless to say, this Okie was not accustomed to swimming in large, natural bodies of water. I liked to swim in concrete pools, where the pH level is tested, and the only living things are people, not snakes, like water moccasins, sea urchins, sharks, or any other potential critter that might swim by and touch my leg. Also in such pools, I am never more than an arm's length from safety. Drowning? Post-meal cramp? Exhausted arms!?! Oh God! GULP! GASP! (Flail.) Oh wait, I can just reach over right here and grab the side. Whew! To me, the sea, under its tranquil surface, is a rippling graveyard, a salty cauldron of death, filled with danger and fear.

Of course to Dalmatians the sea is everything. Those salty waters are the region's lifeblood. The culture, diet, economy, and traditions, all depend on the sea, and have done so for millennia. I mean the center of Split is built around a nearly 2,000-year-old palace, that Diocletian built right on the sea! The traditional songs are filled with heartfelt passion about the sea and nothing but the sea, or maybe some things dealing with the sea, like seagulls, rocks, and um…salt?

People on the coast will attribute all kinds of things to the sea. I think that they think it's magic. Like when Vana had a summer cold, her answer was to swim in the sea. If you have a headache swim in the sea. Or when my friend Mate needed to meet me somewhere at seven in the morning and was planning on going out the night before (going out in Croatia often lasts until 7 a.m.), he said:

When I'm by the sea I never need to sleep.

And he was right. He was right on time and fully alert, and remained so for the rest of the day.

So, there I was on the precipice of marrying into Croatian and Dalmatian culture anxious about the thing most everyone in the region and its visitors loved the most. As a result, I preferred to spend most of my time in the apartment, under the air conditioner, watching movies on TV. Inside I was questioning everything: Were there a plethora of other cultural differences lying under the calm surface of my relationship with Vana? What if I never liked the sea? How could we survive the turbulent waters of matrimony, when I couldn't even swim in the fucking Adriatic? Solution: Fight fear with MORE FEAR. Vana arranged for us to go sailing. Greeeaaaat!

Through a friend we were invited to spend the day on a small sailboat. The Captain was a real *Splićan*, meaning his family had lived in Split since the 1500s. He was probably in his early 60s, a bit plump, but tanned and animated. Just looking at him you thought S-E-A. Before setting out, I stipulated that I needed a life jacket. Laughter. No, I'm serious. I'm NOT GOING ON A SAILBOAT WITHOUT A LIFE JACKET! If my six months in the Cub Scouts taught me anything it was the motto: Be Prepared! And I was preparing for the worst. After some more laughter, some Croatian and gesturing in my general direction, more laughter and a pleading look from Vana, the Captain disappeared below deck. Sounds of heavy rummaging rose above and a few minutes later he returned with a bright orange life vest, covered in a thick layer of dust and still wrapped in its original cellophane. This thing was R-E-T-R-O: bright orange fabric wrapped around giant foam blocks with a some cord you were supposed tie to something. It looked like it was from 1975. The Captain tossed it to me, but asked that I avoid opening it, saying:

Everyone else giggled. With me clutching to the packaged life vest like it were an orange baby, we set sail, the Captain, his wife, Marko, Vana and my terrified self, slipping out of the harbor and making a circuit around Kaštela Bay.

Now, I'm pretty sure that the Captain was purposely trying to terrify me. And enjoying it. The boat went sideways, seemed to bounce in the surf, and tossed us all around. At one point while we were on a collision course for a huge container ship, he explained, turning completely toward me and Vana, that heading toward the ship is actually the international signal for telling them you won't hit it. Then his wife began frantically punching him. A string of Croatian curses flew out of her mouth. And I thought, *we are gonna die.*

We dodged the ship and slowed down. The Captain began talking about the boat. He discussed her like she was part of the family. Telling us about the first day he saw her, how he bought her, took care of her, repairing her for a year, getting her ready for the water, raising her. I suspected there were family photos on the mantle with the Captain lovingly embracing his wife and children and in the right-hand corner, nearly overshadowing the whole family, the bow of his boat. He probably made jokes to his kids about Debra, the ship: Oh well, she's is your wooden sister! Hahahahaha, Daaar! (Before grandkids, my mom did the very same thing with her dogs.) But then, I saw how much he loved his boat and understood that he would never really do anything to put her in real danger. At some point all of my fear left me. I unclenched my fists from their death grip of plastic wrap and foam, and watched the world sail by.

We were married in a small civil ceremony near the beach, Bačvice. Only family were invited, but most of the neighbors came too. We sat in two big chairs while the officiant said a lot of Croatian that I didn't understand. It's funny to be sitting at your wedding, because we don't sit at weddings in the U.S., and not understand a word that's being said. What was I doing? What were we doing? Was this all a hopelessly optimistic mistake? I glanced at Vana. She was visibly nervous. Wide-eyed and nearly panicked. First our hands found each other, then our eyes met and we held our gaze just for a heartbeat. And that was enough, we were both ready to jump.

The Captain harbored us near Kašuni. The sky had turned overcast and it gently began to rain. First Marko jumped into the water. Then Vana followed. Before I knew what I was doing, I leapt too. On the surface the rain was cold, but the sea was warm. Bobbing with my head just above the surf, the mountain Marjan looming above us, the Dinaric Alps cutting the horizon, islands dispersing into the rainy distance, and Vana treading calmly beside me, I no longer felt any fear. I felt sure.

CHAPTER 7

Friendship

In Croatian the word for both foreigner and stranger is *stranac*. Growing up in America, I was always taught to fear strangers, otherwise I would end up missing and my picture would end up on the back of a milk carton. This type of fear was never carried over to foreigners. Sure, I was scared of the Russians, but not because I thought they were going to kidnap me. In order to protect ourselves against persons unknown we had little phrases like "stranger danger" and secret emergency passwords that only family members and trusted friends knew. Ironically, despite all the fear we have for strangers, in the U.S. the line between stranger and acquaintance is not that difficult to cross. And the line between being acquaintances and then friends is even thinner. In Croatia however, I was learning it was nearly impossible to shed my foreignness. And so, even among my wife's friends and acquaintances I was very much still a stranger.

Whenever we met people for coffee I was largely ignored, sometimes with mild indifference and at other times with what felt like simmering scorn. I understand that I didn't speak Croatian, and so it was normal that a lot of the conversation rolled on right past me, but there were occasions when I was purposely left out of the loop. In some situations I was like an exhibit, a real live American on display. Look, but don't touch.

One time we went to see my wife's friend in a small town outside of Zadar. Some of her friend's friends showed up and I happened to have a bottle of Coke in my coat pocket. At one point I took it out and had a drink. A certain female friend remarked how of course the American has Coca-Cola in his pocket. (Bwa-ha-ha. Funny, right? Sure. Well. A. little.) Everyone laughed, and trying to be a good sport, I noted that in the other pocket I also had a Big Mac (which I didn't). Nothing. Silence. No acknowledgment that anything had been said. Just nervous glances the other way. O-K-A-Y. Apparently, I was not allowed to join in making fun of myself (which I believe I happen to be very good at). The rest of the afternoon passed on with no one talking to me, asking me anything or even noting my existence. No one showed the least bit of interest in who I was, other than that I was an American that predictably carried Coke around in his pocket.

There was a very real, though invisible barrier between me and Croatia's social world. I was a foreigner, a stranger, and to be able to move from such a category into a more familiar one was proving to be incredibly difficult. For an American, it was especially difficult.

In the U.S. it is pretty easy to make friends. We move around so much that we develop the ability to enter into friendships effortlessly. In Oklahoma, in New Orleans, in Montreal, in Istanbul I always had people, soon after moving anywhere, that I could call friends. We weren't best friends, but we were friends. Usually, it just takes two or more people liking the same kind of stuff. If you like *Star Wars* and I like *Star Wars* (excluding Episodes I–III, because no one should ever like those) then we are already on the road to friendship. Add some time and frequency and BOOM:

☆Friends☆

But then, over more time, you move away to another place, transfer to another school, decide that you DO like the early *Star Wars* episodes and gradually, eventually drift away from your friend. Friendship in America is easy come, easy go.

Friendship in Croatia is not as fluid as in America, nor is it as fickle. It's thick. It's lasting. It's work. It's also the opposite to our atomized, individualistic lifestyle in the U.S. I feel like in America we run from being responsible to each other. We avoid any and all social burdens. We split the ticket. We keep everything in a balanced equilibrium. So, to call someone friend simply means we like them. This is what I didn't understand in those early months in Croatia. It wasn't that Vana's friends didn't like me, they didn't even seem interested *in* liking me.

The first month we lived in Istanbul one of Vana's friends wanted to come and visit, along with her five-year-old kid. Now, I was not too keen on having guests in a city and country I had just moved to, nor was I happy about having a five-year-old, whose language I didn't speak, come stay with us for a proposed two weeks. I asked Vana if she could at least postpone the trip until we settled in a bit more. *No. No? No.* She wouldn't even ask and there was no way she would tell her friend that she couldn't come. *No? NO! What?* **FRIENDSHIP IN CROATIA:** When you live in a strange country and your friend wants to visit with her kid and despite the objections from your future husband, you still can't/won't say no, or even maybe later.

If this is the power of friendship, then you can imagine why people are choosy about whom they call a friend. Being someone's friend in Croatia basically means you can never, ever, say no to that person, regardless of what she asks of you. You might want to, but all you can do is list all the reasons why you should say no, and then you'll still say yes anyway, because hey: it's your friend. This involves everything from helping someone find work, to giving them discounted prices on things, editing their long academic papers, editing the English version of their novel, having coffee, to letting them stay with you at inopportune times, and if you are out of town when they need to stay with you, letting them stay at your place anyway. All of this is what friends do. Pick the wrong friends and I believe you could end up doing anything, from running cigarettes across the border between Croatia and Bosnia to having indefinite house guests convert your living room to their bedroom.

To penetrate into someone's social circle is not easy, it takes time and several coffees before the bonds of obligation and reciprocity are strengthened enough that someone can or will call you a friend. When I figured all of this out, I was at first repulsed, thinking that everyone was just friends with each other as a means of getting favors. I saw it all as *quid pro quo*. But, this was entirely too cynical. The initial attraction, the shared mutual interests, the synchronization of personality also needs to be there, but then these seemingly shallow and arbitrary bonds are strengthened through the rigmarole of friendship's deeper customs.

Over time I began to branch out on my own and meet new people. I began forging my own network of acquaintances, and as I became more and more intertwined in this odd social game, I began to enjoy being obligated. Friendship is not a burden to carry, but an intimate weight to hold. And by holding on to each other, you feel that you have more support for life's greater burdens.

CHAPTER 8

Family and Cramped Quarters

While Vana's friends were a cold and distant proving ground for my foreignness, her family was immediately warm and welcoming. And good thing, because for a large part of that summer, her sister, twin nephews, myself, Vana and Vida all lived in a two-bedroom apartment together. Then the cousins came.

The whole gift-giving thing had been a bit weird, I'd adjusted to lunchtime, I was enjoying swimming in the sea, but living in such a small space with so. many. people. was proving to be a huge obstacle on my path to cultural acceptance and eventual conformity. In order to keep sane I found an empty spot on the balcony each night, where I would sit and drink, and smoke, and drink and smoke, until I stumbled off to bed. My drunken stupor, wrapped in a cloud of cigarette smoke was the Croatian version of my own room. I walled myself in with beer, shutting out the rest of the world so I could be alone with my murky, foggy, drunken thoughts.

In America, space is not the final frontier, it's just what we use at home to put a border between ourselves and the rest of our family. I grew up in a two-story, 2,325-square-foot home, with my sister, my mom and my stepfather. I had my own room, my sister had her own room, my parents had their own room. We had a dining room we only used on holidays, a living room we also only used on holidays, and a den that we actually used every day. The house had two and a half bathrooms and a basement. In other words, it was always easy to find a place in that house where someone wasn't.

An abundance of space adds a dynamic to American life that I found missing from my Croatian family: irritation and impatience. We are gifted with the privilege of being able to get annoyed easily by our family's little idiosyncrasies, and then we are able to do something about it, like go to our own room, the next room, or any empty room in the house. Mumbling grandmas, mouth-breathing cousins, blabbing sisters, overly critical mothers, and witty know-it-all brothers all get under your skin, but then you just go to your room, play some Nintendo and let good ol' Dr. Mario give you a prescription for familial harmony. In the U.S., nothing brings the family closer than time apart (usually with a TV) in a separate room.

In Split, I had no such recourse, so I used beer and the balcony. As the summer wore on, I was increasingly amazed at how my new family dealt with each other by not dealing with each other. Once the cousins arrived I thought, *now something will happen.* I mean nine people in a two-bedroom apartment?

In the States there would be blood. But, here, nope. No one seemed to ever be annoyed. No one fought. No one yelled. No one seemed to longly desire to put four walls and a door between herself and everyone else. Beneath the surface there seemed to be an infinite well of patience, but it wasn't because everyone loved each other so much they could never disagree or anything. It's not like we were living in a hippy commune. The family just seemed to be more patient with each other. They were more prone to swallowing the annoyances and letting things slide.

I was especially fascinated with the embodiment of calm in Vana's sister, Ivana. The mother of two seven-year-old twins and a 17-year-old daughter, she lived in another two-bedroom apartment with her husband, children and mother-in-law, yet she never seemed to raise her voice, was clearly not on drugs, and didn't drink on the balcony each night. What was the key to her Zen-like serenity?

One evening I badgered her with a bunch of questions that basically went like this: *Well, from my perspective your life looks like hell, but you're not drinking like I am here on the balcony. In fact, you seem happy. What gives?*

With a little more nuance I asked her what it was like raising two infants in such a small space with another kid, a husband, and his mother-in-law. Since I didn't have any kids at that point, it just seemed impossible to have to spend all your time with so many people. How could you not go crazy? But, Ivana just looked at me with the same calm that she used to deal with everything else and said: "I don't know."

But this utterance did not say that she didn't have the answer, rather it suggested that she never had the question. It was never something that concerned her. Why would it? On my perch on the balcony, I was examining everything from a perspective based on my own expectations and I expected to have a room just for me where I could go and be alone when I wanted to.

Growing up, Vana and her sister didn't have the option of storming off to her room declaring that "life is just soooo unfair." She slept in the living room with her sister. While her parents, and grandparents slept in the other two rooms. Of course teenage declarations of life's injustice, running off and slamming doors is part of the American experience (just watch any sitcom from the 1980s). The common calm in this little apartment was one of the first times I began questioning the American way of life. Any equivalent to the large house with a white-picket fence that I had one day hoped to attain (a house with a couple Toyotas and enough extra space for my comic books and *Star Wars* "collectibles") was losing its pull. Like a satellite off its course, I was beginning to drift from America's cultural orbit. I was beginning to change.

CHAPTER 9

U.S.A.

Now here is something a little strange. After marrying Vana and living in Split for the summer, I moved back to the U.S. while Vana stayed in Croatia. Weird, huh? Well along the way I decided that I needed a Ph.D., but, since we weren't sure in which country we would eventually live and because my research would eventually bring me back to Croatia in order to finish my doctorate, we decided it was best if Vana stayed in Croatia. Yes, finding employment here can be that difficult that we decided to live a couple years apart just so that she could keep her job (and so eventually, people would have to call me Dr. Brown. Just kidding. No one calls me doctor).

Returning to the U.S. after two years in Turkey and a summer in Croatia, threw me into reverse cultural shock. Everything was so big and expansive. The flat vast roads lined with nothing but telephone poles and strip malls, fast food joints, and the pollution of signs, branding the air with their noxious message on the marquees: TRY OUR BLT, VALUE MENU, MCRIB IS BACK, all threatened to push me into an agoraphobic fit. Where was the history? Where was the constraint? I had entered into a neon nightmare. The sprawl spread like a cancer. With new eyes I saw so much of the city, my hometown, as nothing more than streets, wedged between a billion black-topped parking lots, acting like arteries, traffic bleeding out from the city center to the suburbs and shopping malls. Where was the culture? The chaotic grace of the urban center? Cafes? Squares? Pigeons? Statues of important dead people? Tulsa was now a land of empty abundance. There was no longer any there, there.

Where was home? Split? Tulsa? What was once my home was boxed up in the closets and garage of my parents' new house. Yes, during my Balkan interlude they had moved. Gone were the scents and sounds of home. The subliminal triggers of memory that infect a place with familiarity, like the passing scent of an old girlfriend's perfume, had been suddenly replaced by something new and unfamiliar.

The new house was massive, 3,368 square feet. After living in a 538-square-foot apartment in Istanbul and then sharing the two-bedroom apartment with my new in-laws all summer long, the sheer size of my parents' new home threw me into fits of nervous laughter. I walked around the house trying to transpose the apartment in Split over the area of this new abode. Mostly though, I now felt like a guest in what was supposed to be my own home.

On drives at night, cutting across this profuse entity of a town, passing the barren parking lots of all the closed shopping centers, I was hit with a profound loneliness. The bare glow of the fluorescent lights, burning above the black parking spaces and the illumination of each store's sign shining pointlessly to the ends of the night, illustrated the emptiness of life in the Midwest. I realized, I now had more attachment to Vida's apartment in Split than I did to my parents' own house. I was like a deck of cards, reshuffled and now dealt as a different hand.

I missed Vana.

In Lawrence, Kansas, where I moved to work on my doctorate at the University of Kansas, things began to meld and I slowly returned to my American self. I also started learning Croatian. Taking Croatian classes helped bridge the distance between me and Vana. It was like each word and case I learned helped bring me back to her. Our class was taught by a Slovenian and consisted mostly of young undergrads whose parents came from the former Yugoslavia: two Croatians, and a Bosnian Serb. Each versed in their own local dialects that had also become infected with a large amount of English words. The little bit of Croatian I knew had a nice *splitski* twang to it that rounded out the group.

Attending the University made everything more bearable. I saw the vast resources of the U.S. put to the productive pursuit of knowledge. Most importantly though, I became a fellow for

KU's Center for Russian and Eastern European Studies. Being among a group of scholars who had traveled and spent time in all of Central and Southeastern Europe and Russia allowed us all to escape from the hurly-burly of American life. And finally, after all of my travels and adventures in the former Yugoslavia, I became clear on where Russia was and exactly which countries and regions had once been, or still were, Russian.

CHAPTER 10

Croatian Service, Keeping it Real, Really Real

Before my experience in the Balkans, I imagined culture as this vast monolithic identity that defined everything about a place and people. On my return to the U.S. I learned that it is actually small, subtle things that comprise the biggest differences. It's not the big wheels of world views, but rather the nuances of daily life that illuminate the distinctiveness of a group, or people's culture. This became all too apparent to me when, after returning to the U.S., I went out to eat with a friend.

The restaurant was a Mexican-themed place wedged next to the entrance of a shopping mall. It was the kind of place where everyone wore the same outfit and there was a cute cartoon character of a drunken Tequila worm on the sign, shirts, and menus. The whole place felt about as authentic as Cher's face. Little did I know, but I had completely acclimated to the Croatian restaurant experience. Unaware of how accustomed I had become to the Croatian way, I waltzed up to the hostess, completely disarmed and unprepared for the oncoming assault of friendly customer service.

"Hi! Welcome To *Wherevers*! How can I help you?" BOOM! I was already thrown off by the polite assistance. And little did I know, but this was just the opening salvo in a barrage of questions. Like a deer in headlights I nervously replied,

"Uh, we'd like a table."

"GREAT! Do you want to sit inside or outside?"

"Um...inside."

"GREAT!! At the bar, the lounge, the nook or the-other-silly-named-place?" I felt as if I was under investigation. Thrown into some kind of interrogation.

"Uh...I guess in the nook."

"GREEEAT!!! Follow me."

Our hostess sort of bounce-pranced into the "nook," hugging our menus like they were wonderful furry little pets. Then she seated us, smiled and bounced right back to the front of the restaurant. It didn't stop there though. When our waitress came to take our orders, she too was *really* friendly and *really* enthusiastic about the fact that WE were sitting in HER section and that SHE was going to get to wait on US. *WOWEEE! Smiles all around.*

I began to realize that my time among Croatians and in Croatia had taught me to be skeptical of...well...everything. I wasn't encouraged by our waitress's pleasantness. In fact, I found it disturbing. *What's the catch?* I wondered. I nervously looked around to see if there were any signs of some happy-friendly-girl-Zombie plague ravaging the metropolitan area.

Then the *real* interrogation began: "Would you like to know our specials? Would you like a margarita? Flavored? Salt? Large? Small? Do you want french fries, coleslaw, queso, salsa, rice, or beans with that? Flour or corn tortillas? Would you like any starters? Buffalo wings, guacamole, chips-n-dips?"

By the end of my order I was exhausted. After she asked my friend the EXACT same questions she reminded us that her name was Tiffany or whatever, and told us to "just holler" if we needed anything. (Giggles. Smiles. Ponytail-flip. Bounce-prance). Five minutes later she brought our drinks, five minutes after that she asked how we liked our drinks, then she brought us our food, asked how we liked our food, then asked us if we wanted dessert, asked us how we liked our dessert? *AARGH! Is she conducting a survey?* I thought. *ENOUGH already!* Between each question about our food, drinks, and fried ice cream, she would again bounce-prance by and ask a more general: "Everything 'kay?"

I realized that evening that no, everything was not 'kay. I had changed. I. Actually. Preferred. Croatian. "Service" to. What. I. Was. Getting. In. America. Now for us to understand just how shocking this and the ramifications it has for my conversion to Croatian customs, I have to explain what Croatian "service" actually entails.

One of the first times I stepped into a cafe in Croatia, I had to wait until the waiter was done reading a magazine and having a cigarette before he took my order. But, this is to be expected because customer service in Croatia is a lot like dealing with the afterlife. After *eventually* taking your order and bringing you your drink, your waiter disappears like a ghost. As if serving you had been the one task keeping him bound to the mortal world. Delivered, he fades into the beyond.

Or sometimes, you, the customer, are the ghost. In Split, this impossible-to-miss big, beefy, muscular waiter came to take our order and didn't even say anything. Or look at us. He actually did everything in his power NOT TO LOOK at us. He just sort of grunted when I ordered, hardly acknowledging that he and we existed on the same dimensional plane (see, just like we were ghosts!).

But now, back at *Wherevers* I was realizing that I prefer to be ignored over being harassed. I preferred the honesty of the Croatian customer/waiter relationship. I am here to drink coffee. You are here because it's a job. Let's not pretend we LOVE it!

Drinking my margarita and munching on tortilla chips between Tiff's bounce-prance interruption, it dawned on me why people from other countries see us as superficial and fake. Was the whole politeness here at *Wherevers* a charade? Was it all just so I would leave Tiff (I don't think she'll mind if I call her Tiff) a good and decent tip? In part yes, but also no. Part of the service industry requires that you be nice and friendly and helpful to your customers. This is the role of the service provider (I know I've been there) and it comes with the job. The incentive for tip helps ensure the smiles stay on your face near the end of an eight-hour split shift.

Still, after my time abroad, Tiff's friendly attitude, enthusiasm and concern wore me out. I'm sure Tiff is a nice person, but she's not THAT nice. I doubt she walks down the street going: NICE TO SEE YOU! I'm GLAD YOU'RE HERE! WOOHOO to everyone she sees. Does she bounce-prance at home? Or when she gets off work? Don't forget, at *Wherevers* we were complete and total strangers with unlikely odds that we would ever see each other again! She told me her name and was really nice just because it was her job. It was an illusion, and once I could see it as such, its disingenuous reality became alienating. I came to see my Croatian waiter's total indifference to my needs as less offensive than the service I had at *Wherevers*. We don't need to pretend we are friends when we aren't, and you don't have to harass me with hospitality. (And the only person *really* authorized to harass you with heavy-handed kindness when you're eating is your Croatian-mother-in-law! Fact.) After I moved back to Croatia I began going to some cafes regularly and eventually the waitstaff's icy indifference faded. We started to talk, and came to casually know each other. Best of all, I know that these conversations are genuine, no one is being nice in hopes of getting a bigger tip, because waiters in Croatia, they keep it real, really real.

SPLIT ★ PART 2

CHAPTER 11

Split

I always wondered how Diocletian's Palace became the center of Split. Built in the 4th Century A.D. the palace served as the Emperor's retirement home. And I doubt he said: *Hey, everybody, let's make a city!* In fact the palace was left abandoned after the fall of Rome, but at some point the countryside's residents eventually moved in and made it their own, meaning that someone at sometime must have had a conversation like this:

> Former Roman Peasant 1: Hey, Buddy. You know what?
> Former Roman Peasant 2: No? What?
> FRP1: I'm tired of living in this…err…hut or whatever it is we live in.
> FRP2: So? *(Shrugs)*
> FRP1: So? SO, *(putting his arm around his interlocutor)*, there is a perfectly good, hardly-been-used palace, just sitting over that yonder hill.

>FRP2: *(In thoughtful repose, finger touching chin, eyes skyward)* Hey, now you're talking. I mean, why should we be living in these awful, whatever-they-ares, when we could be living it up in a bonafide PAL-ACE.
>FRP1: Word.

And then I guess they loaded the kids onto their donkeys, packed up their...*um*...things, and moved to Split.

Now, some millennium and a half later, I too moved to Split, but only came with a suitcase and arrived on an airplane. I also didn't move into the palace, but rather lived with Vana in Vida's socialist-era apartment just outside the center. Of course the funny thing about Split (and Dalmatia for that matter) is how the modern world's borders are buttressed by antiquity. In other once ancient places, like Istanbul, Cairo, and Rome, the past is but an obstruction to the present, an obelisk in the way of progress, some ruins in the middle of the road. These artifacts of history are slowly consumed by the rush of traffic and exhaust, devoured by the newer relics of the industrial age. So too, is the culture and lifestyle that once went with them. But, in Split, it is different. Split still as a whole, has a certain pace that serves as a lull, a lethargic gait that moves in such a counter-rhythm to the modern world, that you know it is the true bridge of continuity between the present and the past. Life in Split, like the walls of Diocletian's Palace seems to stubbornly resist the new.

The way people live doesn't really seem that different than how they must've lived centuries ago. Vida still preferred to shop at the open-air market every morning rather than at the grocery store. Every morning she trudges back to apartment, burdened with the ingredients for the day's lunch, regional cheese, locally grown *blitva,* fish caught just off the coast. Along the quay old men stroll in groups, their hands clasped behind their backs, their brows furrowed in conversation. A nun skirts by a narrow passage inside the palace. Church bells ring for sext, the midday mass. Lunch comes and the center empties of everyone, but a few lonely tourists. With evening comes coffee and an evening swim. As dusk settles the traffic snakes from the coast back into the town, and at night the neighbors gather and gossip under the eaves of the balcony.

Was it really that different 100, 200, 1,000 years ago? Even outside the ancient city center, where the Vespas sputter through the night and pop music bounces from passing cars like discarded litter, you sense that these are only intermittent modern-day distractions. Lying in the summer heat you know it is the same heat, graced with the same sense of the sea, that Diocletian must have felt when he slept at night. The air is steeped with the same scents of pine, lavender and rosemary, that those seeking refuge from the Vandals, Vars and Visigoths, a millennia ago knew was the smell of home.

Even though I had been back and forth to Croatia several times and spent the summer in Split, I was still enticed by the prospect of living in an exotic, former Communist, war-ravaged country. On moving to Split and to Croatia for good, I still believed life in Croatia would be something like the *Bourne Identity*. Guess what? Life in Croatia is NOTHING like the *Bourne Identity*.

I had this realization when shopping with Vida for some shoes in Kaštela on my birthday. Yep, looking at shoes with your mother-in-law on your b-day is about as far from the action-adventure genre as one can get. If living in the Balkans wasn't going to be a "three-out-of-four stars" "first-rate thriller" or "a rollicking adventure yarn" with a "strong performance by Matt Damon," then what was life here going to be like? I didn't know, but it was only after coming back that I think, I began to see Croatia as it actually was, and not what I had imagined it would be.

CHAPTER 12

Neighbors

Back on that first trip to Split, I came down with a terrible head cold. Feverish, I sprawled on the couch, watching reruns of *Murder She Wrote*. I think Vida was worried I was going to die, and then she would have an international incident on her hands. No one wants a dead American. She repeatedly asked Vana if I should see the doctor. I felt that this was completely unnecessary and with enough cold medicine, I would be fine. But she kept insisting, and insisting. Little did I know, but the doctor was actually an upstairs neighbor. So, by "see the doctor," she meant having the neighbor come down and examine me, which she did.

Adorned with a stethoscope around her neck and a paper bag filled with a thermometer and tongue depressor and other medical instruments, the neighbor gave me a typical check-up: breathe in, breathe out, cough, say ahhh, and her hands searched my neck. She spoke to Vana in lightning-fast Croatian while doing all this. And then she turned to me.

Diagnosis:

"You have a cold."

Prognosis:

"You will get better faster if you take this bag of lemons I'm giving you, put them, and this bottle of homemade alcohol that I am also giving you, in some tea and drink it, regularly."

Right. So a neighbor doctor just came by, examined me, and gave me a gift of strong alcohol. *Where was I? Fucking Mayberry?* This was something that we only saw in America on TV shows from the 1950s, when I guess stuff like this actually happened.

Welcome to the neighborhood. Welcome to the wonderful world of Croatian neighbors.

Vida's apartment was on the second floor of a drab, five-story walk-up that epitomized the gray-crushing soullessness of socialist housing, as it was essentially one giant concrete block with no architectural grace or charm. It didn't scream as much as mutter utility, rather than design. Flanked by a park littered with the detritus of cigarette butts, beer caps, and dog poop, the other side of the building housed a lunar cragged parking lot with too few spaces and too many rundown cars from Yugoslavia. It was the kind of place that even on sunny days could look overcast. But, the bland conformity of the exterior was completely misleading to the unique color and warmth of the building's inhabitants.

The neighbors in Split were more like extended family than the random residents of the same building. The familiarity with everyone, the random comings and goings, the uncanny ability for everyone to seemingly know everything about you before you've even said anything, was something I was not at all prepared for.

IN THE U.S. WE HAVE AN EXPRESSION:
Good fences make good neighbors.

And we live by it. Our houses have fences, sometimes for aesthetics, sometimes for privacy. For those of us that live in apartments we purposely avoid each other, hurrying to open the door and get inside when we hear our neighbor coming down the hall. Anything to avoid getting stuck in an awkward, hi or hello. There is generally a mutual understanding that my business is none of your business and your business is none of my business. The ever-present nosy neighbor is a nearly extinct specimen, now only found in sitcoms and Hollywood films.

THE CROATIAN VERSION OF THIS PROVERB IS PROBABLY SOMETHING LIKE THIS:

Thin walls, echoey corridors, and open windows, make…neighbors.

The idea of privacy from the neighbors is laughable. It's not so much that the neighbors have prying eyes and ears as it is they have *eyes* and *ears*. Things are heard, and known without anyone willfully trying to hear and know them. Because of the noise, you know what shows your upstairs neighbor watches each night. You know when the teenagers in the building come home drunk in the early morning, laughing about this or that romantic exploit. You know who is sick, who's not, who's working, who's not. Rather than run from this situation, it is just accepted. The shared awareness of each other among the neighbors fosters a stronger sense of community than what I had experienced in my adult life in the U.S. The bond between neighbors extends beyond the proximity of the apartment building and into all other parts of Croatia. The building or street that makes you neighbors is like its own country and the sons and daughters of neighbors, even if they now live in Zagreb, Italy, or Germany are your fellow citizens. Calling someone *susjed* can almost be like calling them a cousin.

In Split, the neighbors' and our doors were open almost at all times of the day. One Christmas Eve, just after I arrived from the States, Vana and I just came to Split from Zagreb at 11:30 p.m., and Vida mentioned that we should go see what the neighbors were up to and wish them a Merry Christmas. In Oklahoma it would be very, very unusual to go over to the neighbors' house on Christmas Eve at 11:30 at night with your daughter and son-in-law. Like almost-get-shot kind of unusual. Nevertheless, we walked across the hall and sure enough, the neighbors were up and they of course invited us in. Somehow or another we got to talking about Russia and America, and who has more soul. The Croatians said, clearly the Russians. And I said, *What am I doing here talking about the Russian soul on Christmas in Croatia?* Then the neighbors tried to show me how their dog can sing, but we all had to sing first. So between more examples of Russia's soul and America's soullessness, our hosts belted off a few bars of humming followed by the silent anticipation of their dog joining along. When the dog failed to sing, we were all encouraged to hum, even though we ended up all humming completely different songs. More! More! Our hosts hands enthusiastically encouraged. Louder! More! Still nothing. The dog's eyes met mine and we shared a moment, a bond of equal bewilderment, both of us looking lost. Then the conversation about Russia resumed.

The neighbors also look out for each other. While Vana and I were living in Istanbul, Vida was very ill and lay bedridden for a week or more. During that time, it was the neighbors who took care of her. Every morning the neighbor, Paula, brought her breakfast and the newspaper. For lunch, the neighbor across the hall came over with a cooked meal. And the doctor upstairs came down with dinner and some company each evening.

Of all the neighbors, Paula was the most intuitive to who needed help and when. When Vida left us for three days to go pick olives on the island of Korčula, Paula appeared every day, like magical clockwork, with lunch for Sara (our daughter, see the next chapter about that). The mother of three sons and the grandmother of three granddaughters, Paula is one of the most generous people on the planet. She is a fixture to Vida's as much as me or Vana ever are. She comes without a knock, but just enters, sometimes for a specific reason, other times just to see what's going on, most of the time with a plate full of food. She's like a reverse Kramer from *Seinfeld,* never far, nearly always there, but instead of taking food, she brings it. Crepes at midnight, fish, *blitva*, pizza, or tripe for lunch, she cooks all of it and brings all of it over for anyone to try. When she doesn't feel like coming over, she uses her broom to bang on the railing of our balcony from her balcony. Usually, to ask if we want something she's cooking, or if we've read the paper yet.

But, what really makes Paula, Paula is that with all of her loving generosity and concern about everyone's well-being is a string of curse words that precedes or follows anything she says. These phrases generally involve fornicating with your mother and would make any American grandmother's hair stand on end. Anytime I pass on eating something she's cooked, she says: *Aye, fuck your mother!* Or *dick!* Anytime I thank her for something she's cooked, she dismisses my gratitude with an indifferent frown, followed by *fuck your mother*. And most memorably, when my daughter was born she proclaimed: *You are the most beautiful girl in the world! Fuck your mother!*

The relationship between neighbors is one of the most valuable things Croatia has going for it. It's crazy, annoying, but also comforting to know that everyone else knows what you are up to, what you need, and who you are. Being integrated into such a community is something uncommon for Americans. It's something we talk about from the past. And sure, if it weren't for all the cursing, drinking and dog singing, the neighborhood in Split would be like something from a 1950s television show, but with much, much more color. What it really shows is how here people still rely on one another, whereas in the U.S., at least in the places I've lived as an adult, we are all trying to live on our own little island.

CHAPTER 13

Baby

Remember all that I said about Vana and I having some kind of special connection, something celestial and guided by fate, something that was massively bigger than ourselves? (If not, you might need to go back and read chapters 1 and 2. It's cool, I'll wait.) We decided to put all of it to the test and have a baby. If the baby grew up to be a great person, then all of the sacrifice we had made, me leaving my family and country, Vana putting up with me, me learning an incredibly difficult language, well, then all of that would be worth it (no pressure, sweetie). So one weekend, we got some time to ourselves and well you know how it goes (if not, then maybe you should go take a biology class or read a bit more on the internet). In any case, nine months later beautiful Sara was born on a beautiful February morning in Split, because almost every morning in Split is beautiful, EVEN in FEBRUARY.

Now, if you really want to understand the importance of culture, and how there are vast, though subtle differences between cultures, I mean if you really want to get up to your neck in *culture,* why then you should have a baby in a foreign country. Yep, there is nothing like raising a kid in a place far from home to put a spotlight on what you and your wife, mother-in-law, neighbors, sister-in-law, OK all the in-laws, as well as total strangers differ about when it comes to your child's well-being.

After Sara was born my life in Croatia drastically changed, not because I now had to deal with dirty diapers and someone needing my attention all the time. That part of parenthood was fine, even fun. No, my life changed because everything I did that was my American way of doing things, now threatened not only my own life, but apparently the life of my daughter. But let's back up a bit first. Rewind.

In the nine months before we had our baby, having a baby was a terrifying idea. Without any conscious effort I kept remembering everything I had ever accidentally broken. The canopy on my X-wing at age four. The arm of my Darkseid action figure at age five. The screen of my dropped Game Boy at age 12. The car I wrecked at age 16, and again at 19. A lifetime of snapped pencils, cracked cassette tapes, chipped CDs, shattered glasses, plates, and mugs. The utterly destroyed snow globe from Christmas '87. A few windows. And even my own sternum. At night, next to Vana, with our daughter growing in her womb, I laid in bed worried that I could somehow, "break" our baby just like all those other things I'd broken in the past. I knew that I knew nothing about being a father.

But, my self-doubts were assuaged by knowing that we wouldn't be alone. We would be surrounded by years of experience. Not only from Vida, but also from the neighbors. They, I believed, would help guide us and tell us what to do. They would give us some solid parenting advice.

WARNING!
WARNING!

UNDERSTATEMENT!
UNDERSTATEMENT!

It turns out that once you have a baby in Croatia, everyone, and I mean EV-ERY-ONE is full of not just advice, but downright demands, orders, commands, dictates. Grandmas, aunts, neighbors, cousins, total and complete strangers will tell you, with little embarrassment or apology, what you are doing wrong.

On one warm, beautiful day in mid-June, I was sitting on a bench holding our four-month-old daughter, just watching the world go by. It was the kind of day I would later dream about in Zagreb in January. Sunny. Warm. Perfectly still. Temperatures in the mid 20s. Sara was content, making sounds and watching the trees. And well, here comes an old lady half-hobbling down the sidewalk. Dressed all in black, a clear sign that she was a widow, and with a dark scarf covering her hair I could tell she was of the old school, like Hapsburg old. Now, in the recent months I had learned that holding a baby is like holding a people magnet. Everyone will come talk to you when you have a baby, anywhere. Once people saw me with a baby, they had to come smile, make little cooing noises for the baby, and say something to me about the baby. And so, here on this bench, I prepared myself for the inevitable: smiles, laughter and Croatian words like *slatkica, slatka* or something to do with the word *slatko, sweet*.

As the old woman got closer I saw the smile begin to form on the corners of her mouth. Slowly her lips curved upward, her eyes began to sparkle and crinkle as a parabola of happiness spread across her face…Then it stopped. In less than an instant her eyes widened with deadly seriousness. Her smile vanished, replaced by a sinister-looking frown. She stopped just before us, her presence now wrapped in the air of offense. Next thing I know there is all this finger wagging, head shaking, and a bunch of rapid, angry Croatian. *Croatian Croatian Croatian Croatian Croatian Croatian finger wag wag wag wag, Croatian Croatian Croatian, gesture to the world around us.* And I'm sitting there with my head sideways, like *huh? What'd I do?* Maybe she couldn't see us that well, so I held Sara a little higher: *Ba-by, see, ba-by. Cute?* No use. The rant went on.

I was finally able to make out what the woman was getting at. The source of her rage was my careless fathering. There I was, sitting with my daughter on a beautiful day, outside, and she wasn't wearing any socks! And she had short sleeves on. At one point the woman told me she must wear socks. I nodded and then replied with my usual: *don't blame me, blame America,* by telling her I was an American. And that did it. She looked at me with utter disbelief and a hint of disgust, muttered a *Bože moj* and went on her way, leaving the negligent father and abused child to their own devices. I'm sure that later she lit a candle for my daughter's sock-less soul.

The community in Croatia is so strong that neighbors and even strangers have no problem intervening in the upbringing of your child. Now to many people the idea of total strangers approaching me and telling me how to raise my kid is intrusive, offensive and at least a little bit annoying. You might be less impressed by a neighbor being able to smack your kid (that story is in the next paragraph). But, I like it. Um…not so much the hitting part, but the idea that everyone can be involved in what you're doing. Hillary Clinton said that someone somewhere in Africa once said that to raise a child it takes a village. In Croatia it apparently takes your in-laws, neighbors, friends, and total strangers to raise a kid. In a world where we all seem to be more and more introverted and isolated from the physical and social world around us, I love that an old lady cares enough about my daughter's bare feet to let me have it.

One of the neighbor's sons, Ante, told me a story from the war. In 1991, at the beginning of the War in Croatia the air raid sirens went off in Split. Everyone in the building ran down into the basement, worried that either the Yugoslav Army's naval ships or airplanes were going to bombard the town. But, Ante was just a kid and didn't really understand what was happening. Instead he saw the absence of people and the lack of traffic to be an opportunity to finally ride his bike down the big hill beside the house. Of course his mother was desperately worried over his absence and the possible violence that might rain from above at any minute. Later, after the danger had passed he came walking up just as his mother and the other neighbors were exiting the basement. One of the older men in the building walked up to him and without a word just smacked him across the face. Reflecting on the incident later, Ante explained how important that slap was. It actually showed him how serious the situation was, how upset his mother had been, and how much this neighbor cared about him and his mother. *Even then I knew that I deserved that smack,* he recalled.

In Split my daughter's well-being was on everyone's agenda. One time she was very sick, coughing and crying in the night, with a high temperature. When we had to give her medicine her cries became wails of discomfort and refusal. From the open window of our bedroom to the open windows above and below us, all of the neighbors knew what was happening. The next day each one asked us how Sara was. Tomo, Paula's husband told me how he was just listening to Sara's cries, worried, thinking: *poor, poor Sara.* Then of course everyone gave us advice on what would make her better. Cook this with that, hold her like this, have her drink some of this.

The involvement of everyone in Sara's early months of existence is one my most valued memories about my early life in Croatia. Would it be the same in the U.S.? I don't know. What I do know is in most of the places I've lived, everyone has been in such a transient, temporary period in their life that no one forms these kind of lasting bonds between neighbors. Having the support of the community, has made parenthood easier. Of course, there can be such a thing as too much advice. Especially when this "advice" goes against everything you were taught as a kid, or the very things you enjoy in life, like being barefoot.

CHAPTER 14

The Bare Feet Cry Freedom

Back to the first time I visited Croatia and met Vida, I was greeted at the door with a pair of women's slippers. *Because?* Well, this took me a while to figure out. Since I was coming from Istanbul I was used to removing my shoes before entering the house, but that was a custom supported by religious dictates. I eventually figured that Croatia must be like Japan and people like to keep the house clean by removing their shoes. Alright, so that's half of the equation: in Croatia people take their shoes off indoors. Now for the other half: the slippers.

Prior to arriving in Split I had no idea that being barefoot can cause all kinds of illnesses. I was later to learn that walking around, sometimes even in socks, is a good way to get rheumatism, the flu, the common cold and bladder infections (or so I'm told. And frequently!). The first line of defense in the battle for healthy feet are the *papuče* or slippers. What made this even more confusing is the fact that what people were wearing as slippers were not really slippers at all. In the U.S. a slipper or "house shoe" is generally something soft, fuzzy, pink and or made of manly flannel. And we prefer to call them house shoes because "slipper" sounds like something from a Disney film (*Aladdin* and *Cinderella* wear "slippers," in 'Merica we 'Mericans wear house shoes!) In Croatia, a "slipper" is sometimes a slipper of the fuzzy kind, but more often it's a sandal, a pair of flip-flops, any kind of open shoe, even a pair of Crocs (which is ironic because the only time a Croatian would wear Crocs is inside. Period.).

So, when Vida handed me a pair of women's sandals that first night I was in Croatia, I wore them out of politeness for about five minutes before kicking them off and strolling around in my socks. Then my feet seemed to pick up an echo. With each step I heard a voice say: *Ti si bos* (you are barefoot). *Ti si bos,* in the living room. *Ti si bos,* in the kitchen. *TI SI BOS! BOŽE MOJ!* on the balcony.

This concern over my bare feet was in sharp contrast to how I was raised in America. As a kid, one of the best days of the year was when the temperature first hit 72° F. That meant we could kick off our shoes and run around, not just inside, but OUTSIDE, barefoot! There was nothing better than sitting on the porch and stripping off your stinky, sweaty socks and shoving them into your Buster Brown tennis shoes. Your toes wiggled in gratitude. They were free! You were free! It was summer! (Inspiring music plays, swelling with emotion, growing into a crescendo of celebration! Arms raised in triumph, let's go run around barefoot…)

Errrrk! Stop the music. You live in Croatia now. There will be no bare feet. *Even in the summer? Even. In. The. Summer.* Even in a place like Split, a place with palm trees and a sea for God's sake, you have to have your feet covered at all times. *But…um…*

What is even more confusing is how the one place Americans think we should never go barefoot is the one place Croatians insist we go barefoot: at the sea side. On the coast, when I want to wear my Crocs into the water there is some amused laughter and embarrassment in the eyes of my Croatian companions (my wife rolls her eyes). Pointy rocks? Yes. Sea urchins? Sometimes. Wearing shoes to protect my feet from those things? NEVER!

Now that we were living in Split the difficulty came in explaining how integral being barefoot is to life in America. We have apple pie, McDonald's, air-conditioned summers, big cars, and yes, we go barefoot inside all year and outside on the warm days. In the U.S., bare feet are free feet.

Vida, Vana, everyone, seemed to believe I was just lazy or lying or something. My explanations of how things were "in my country" were greeted with looks of severe skepticism and shocked appall. And yet, truly, some of my dearest memories of childhood are about being barefoot. Even today I can still recall the specific bumpy cracks and crags I felt underfoot when running down the length of my driveway. At night, when I can't sleep I try remember how the floors in certain rooms felt to my feet when I was a kid. The carpet in my bedroom, the carpet in my parents' room, the wooden floor of the hallway, the cold tile in the bathroom and the squares of sunlight streaming through the windows, resting on the dining room rug. I could walk my childhood blind if I could walk it barefoot.

As Sara grew from a baby to a toddler I watched her and was reminded of my childhood and in what become an increasingly complicated goal, I wanted to let her share the same sensations I had as a kid. I thought she should be able to be barefoot every now and then. Inside and outside! Of course when I traipsed around the apartment in my bare feet, the Croatians (relatives and some neighbors) looked at me like I was a mad man who wandered out into oncoming traffic. Considering all the ailments that can come from exposed feet, my bare feet were loaded guns and I was playing Russian roulette. Gambling with my life was fine. I think there was even some hope that I would be stricken with some horrible disease just so I could learn a lesson, but when I wanted to let Sara walk around barefoot, that was a different matter. One that broke one of the covenants of *Bakadom:*

THY GRANDCHILD'S FEET SHALL NEVER BE BARE!

Then Sara sort of the took the initiative herself. As she got older she would ask me: *Daddy, why do you walk around barefoot, but momma doesn't?* How could I respond? *Well, as far as I'm concerned your mom and grandma believe in a bunch of made up illnesses that you can somehow get from being barefoot.* Instead I opted for something like this: *Well, I am an American so I can walk around barefoot.* (Did I ever imagine that I would be in a situation where I defined being American as someone who doesn't regularly wear socks or slippers indoors? Um. No.)

A few weeks later we were at the park with all the other neighborhood kids. It was a warm day in May. Sara was playing in the sandbox. I sat with the other children's grandmas on a nearby bench. Sara ran up to me and asked if she could take her shoes off and play in the sandbox. I said sure. She promptly removed her sneakers and socks and shoved her socks back inside her shoes. She wiggled her toes in delight, letting the sand sift through them. Everything was fine until the other kids got wind of what she was doing. Then, like a group of beseeching peasants they asked their grandmas if they could take their shoes off too. Of course the answer was NO! I was confronted with angry stares from the now disgruntled grandmas. They began speaking Croatian really fast, a clue they were talking about me. The kids protested, asking why can Sara be barefoot if they can't. I raised my hand beginning to offer some bit of an excuse, when Sara turned to all of them and said: *It's OK. I'm an American.*

What more could we say?

The concern of bare feet was the least of our problems. There is another, greater more divisive cultural difference between Americans and Croatians. One that involves a truly silent killer…the wind!

CHAPTER 15

Propuh, the Murderous Wind

There was something strange about wind in Croatia that I couldn't quite put my finger on. In the summer, I would open a window at one end of the apartment, and then open another one at the other end, in order to take in the nice mountain breeze blowing off of the Dinaric Alps, but then someone would immediately jump up and hurriedly shut one the windows. On the hottest nights I would sleep with an oscillating fan blowing on me, but then, in the early morning hours Vida would come into the room and turn the fan off. All the while shaking her head in bewildered disgust.

Well, it turns out, Croatians are terrified of the breeze. More specifically, by any breeze indoors. Outside airflow is moderately safe. Indoor airflow is deadly.

WELCOME TO THE WONDERFUL WORLD OF PROPUH.

Huh? Pro-what? Right. The closest thing Americans have for this word is draft, but this alone is deficient in explaining the cultural (and medical) importance of *propuh* in any way. In English a draft is defined as a current of cool air in a confined space. The end. *Propuh* on the other hand is the scourge of Croatian grandmas. This dastardly, and yes, at times deadly, draft, this awful form of airflow is associated with all sorts of ailments: muscles aches, headaches, backaches, earaches, colds, the flu, bacterial infection of the kidneys, bladder, and spleen, and the most feared of them all, inflammation of the brain. Ladies and gentlemen, dear readers, in short, *Propuh* kills!

IN ORDER TO PRECLUDE SUCH MALADIES IT IS NECESSARY TO:

❶
Immediately dry your hair after a shower.
Never go outside or go to sleep with wet hair.

❷
Never expose the back of your or your child's neck to the wind during the fall, winter or spring. The back of your neck should always be covered with a hood or scarf.

❸
Never go barefoot. Always wear socks and slippers (even during the summer on the coast).

❹

Avoid having two or more windows open in the same room, especially if they are on different walls. The cross-breeze is one of the more nefarious forms of *propuh*.

❺

Always cover your midriff and the vital organs contained therein, so that the breeze can't get to them.

Here are some helpful diagrams to show you the acceptable levels of *propuh* and what to do when those levels exceed the recommended dosage.

PROPUH DANGER LEVEL: MODERATE TO LOW

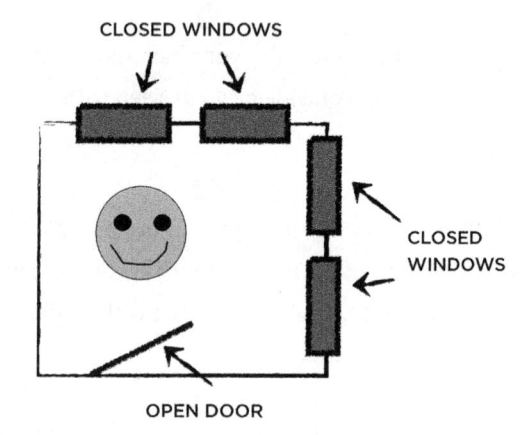

PROPUH DANGER LEVEL: MODERATE TO HIGH

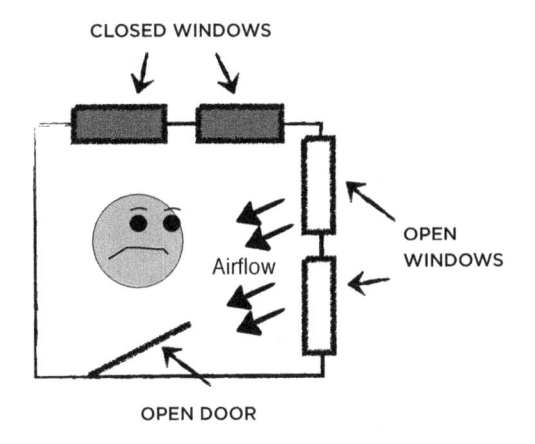

PROPUH DANGER LEVEL: EXTREMELY HIGH!!

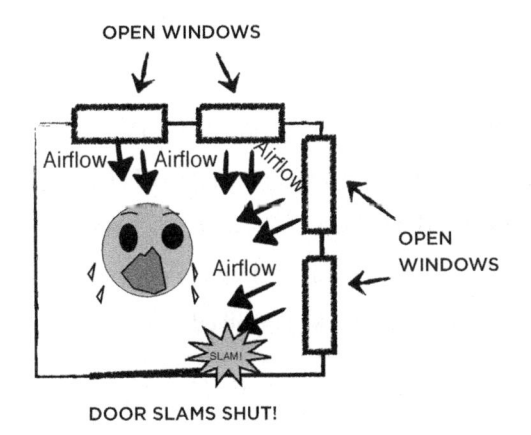

If you should find yourself in a room with an extremely high *propuh* danger level, detecting a cross-breeze, you should: first place your fingers over your ears so that the air doesn't get inside your head and inflame your brain, make sure all socks and slippers are secured firmly on your feet, tuck your shirt and undershirt into your pants (better yet into your *hulahopke*[5]) then as fast as possible, assuming that you are strong enough to move against the gentle air current that is lightly, softly, lithely entering the room, and with all the desperate strength you can muster in what might be your final moments, shut all of the windows!

Apparently there is some kind of American immunity to *propuh*. In fact as an American I have no fear of the draft. None. At. All. In Oklahoma a nice breeze is considered a good thing. Our state song says: OKLAHOMA, *where the wind comes sweeping down the plains*. And that, is considered one of the few positive attributes for the state. This can make for some awkward situations, conversations, and all around complications for an American in Croatia. It's a lot like when I used to talk to evangelizing ultra-Christian teenagers at the pool hall. Like them I believe in God and Jesus, but we didn't really believe in God and Jesus in the same way. They talked about Jesus like he was involved in everything. According

---

5 *Hulahopke* means tights, but it again doesn't real translate because when I hear the word tights I imagine the things ballerinas and superheroes wear. In Croatia, most women, kids, and maybe men wear tights under their pants during the fall, winter, and spring. They are considered one of the great forms of defense against *propuh*.

to these Bible-kids, I would make the shot on the pool table, if, and probably only if, I asked Jesus to help me. If I failed, it was because Jesus had "other" plans for me. Even at 15, I was pretty sure I was not so completely the center of the universe that Jesus stood-in for me during a friendly billiards game. And this is how *propuh* is for me and most Croatians. Yes, I believe in the draft, meaning I feel it, I know it's there, I just don't attribute any potential ailments to its presence. It is only wind and it has no effect on my health, just like Jesus has no influence on my pool game.

See, *propuh* is a force that guides and influences the entire way of life in Croatia. It's why I sweat in the summer. It is why public transport is stifling. Open a window on a tram and you'd think you opened a window on an airplane flying 10,000 meters above the earth. PANIC! *Propuh* is why I am publicly reprimanded for being a bad father when out with my hatless daughter. It is why we have to have extra slippers for guests and pack our own when we go visit someone. And my refusal to accept its existence is why I will forever and always be an outsider.

I need a breeze. There is nothing worse than putting an Oklahoman in a room with stagnant, nonmoving air. I need circulation. I need to feel the wind move across my arms, legs, and face. The breeze to me is like the sea to Dalmatians. I think of the breeze, indoors or outdoors, as always being good. Whenever I meet fellow Americans who have also expatriated themselves to Croatia, we cannot understand how people can believe in the power of *propuh*. We laugh and poke fun at our friends and families' fears of the wind, chalking it up there with other superstitions, like believing in vampires, fairies and Bigfoot. Those of us in mixed marriages end up venting our frustration on our children's relatives who we see as overdressing our kids to death. And this wind-phobia exists all through Southeastern Europe. A friend married to a Bulgarian woman put it best when he said: "In Bulgaria, a sweater is something a kid wears when her mother feels a breeze."

Now that we had a baby the situation became more intense. Vida was soon enacting a zero tolerance for *propuh*. Which meant I was sweating and intolerably uncomfortable all the time. At night I wanted to sleep with the fan on, so I would have to position it just so, in order to make sure it didn't blow on baby Sara or Vana. I had to secretly open the windows and secretly unswaddle my daughter when I saw she was too hot. It is very difficult when two people have the best intentions, but completely different ideas of what is actually the best. We basically settled into a war of attrition, me opening windows, her shutting them, me pulling socks off of Sara, her putting them on. Poor Vana was somehow trapped in the middle and took a more compromising approach. She was the peacemaker, letting me have the last say in the summer, but then agreeing with Vida during all the other months.

Honestly, *propuh* and the slipper thing were and still are two of the most difficult aspects about living in Croatia. A lot of times people don't believe that there are that many (and large) cultural differences between Americans and Croatians. The problem of *propuh* probably is the biggest example of our differences. It shows the enormity of the cultural chasm that exists between us.

Every fiber of my being screams for the wind. I think it is healthy. I want my daughter to be in the wind. She might be half-Croatian, but she is also American! I finally had to use that excuse, saying to Vida, the in-laws, the neighbors, and strangers that she can handle *propuh*, she's American! Whoever thought my slumbering patriotism would be awoken by the wind! Yet, the wind is as American as apple pie. It is an iconic symbol of America, it is what our optimism rides on. In our pantheon of heroes they all sit on horseback, silhouetted against the setting sun, the tall grass beneath them rustling in the breeze and their hair blown back by the wind, ceaselessly.

CHAPTER 16

Fashion

Whenever I would fly back to Oklahoma I felt like I was shedding layers of culture, like a snake sheds skin. The move from Europe to Mid-America always took me from a place where almost everything had an air of elegance, from the small cups of coffee to my finely dressed compatriots flying alongside me, and dropped me in a place where elegance is a word more likely to be mistaken for elephant. At each successive gate, at each successive airport I could tell I was getting closer to home by the decrease in concern for outward appearance and an increase in concern for jumbo-sized everything. Finally, I arrived at the gate for Tulsa, Oklahoma and a little bit of me died inside. Sure it's one step away from home, but it's also filled with people wearing sweatpants, shorts with calf-high white socks, matching his-n-hers Eskimo Joe's shirts, flip-flops, tank tops that hardly hide tufts of armpit hair, and oversized basketball shorts on a pack of slack-jawed yokels. While the U.S. may have our security agencies reading our emails and monitoring our phone calls, one thing we clearly do not have is the fashion police.

Imagine going from Split where you see and laugh at the poorly dressed tourists, to ending up on a plane, then in a state and finally a city filled with them. This was me each time I went home. It wasn't always this way. My first summer in Split I was decked out in my white socks, shorts, and tennis shoes ready to hit the *riva,* the main seaside promenade. I was quickly informed that I was ready to go nowhere. My *punica*[6] forbade (YES! FOR-BADE) me from leaving the house in what I had been leaving the house in my whole life. At the time I thought this was a little repressive. I figured why should this lady care what I wear out. It's not like people on the *riva* will know that I'm her son-in-law (actually, I later learned it is totally like that). I actually believe my mother-in-law was trying to save me from myself. Another time I went to the center in a raggedy old hooded sweatshirt and felt like a homeless man (except homeless men in Croatia are dressed better than this). Feeling out of place by a publicly inadequate level of dress was a new experience for me. In the U.S., anything goes.

Croatians are generally a pretty stylish bunch. Though not everyone dresses or looks the same. There are people

---

6 A note to our American readers, *punica* (pronounced poo-nitsa) is the Croatian word for mother-in-law. As a concept the name mother-in-law just doesn't do it justice, so I have elected to use *punica* throughout the rest of this book.

who dress more alternatively, there are hipsters, punks and goths. There are people who (attempt) to dress stylishly what we would call preps, or trendy folks. There are the super stylish, the fashionistas. And there are *cajkuša*. There is really no translation for *cajkuša*. No matter which style one adopts, people here are dressed with a self-awareness or self-consciousness that demonstrates a commitment to looking good: Stylistically diverse, but stylish nonetheless. Even at the university here I have never seen someone that looks like they just rolled out of bed, slipped on some pants just off the floor and strolled out into the day (that, by the way, is basically how I rolled all through undergrad). Even when my students come in hungover their eyes might look like boiled eggs slathered in Tabasco sauce, but their clothes are ironed.

There is, however, one puzzle piece in the mosaic of Croatian fashion and that is the asymmetrical gender standards. Really. It's not uncommon to see a woman who looks and is dressed like a supermodel at bauMax (the European Home Depot) or wherever with a dude wearing tracksuit pants, a t-shirt and a fanny pack (all still ironed though). I mean this guy is really one pair of white socks away from being an Oklahoman. In America we are equal opportunity eyesores. You can see a man dressed in sweatpants and a t-shirt from a Bible study camp he went to in 1996 and in the same tacky gaze lay witness to a large woman wearing an oversized Tweety Bird t-shirt and a pair of butt-tight turquoise shorts. Those images are just a fact of life. What I don't get about Croatia is how the women often dress like they fell out of the pages of a fashion magazine and the dudes dress like my uncle right after he's mowed the lawn. And they'll be TOGETHER.

Growing up in America I rebelled against the idea that we should have socially imposed norms. This led me to dying my hair and sporting a mohawk (something Croatians call an *iroquois* for some reason). As a result of the counterculture or the fact that we spend most of our time with the television, which can't see what we are wearing, it feels like there are no longer any social demands for how one should look and dress. There was actually a time when men couldn't go outside without wearing a hat! Nowadays we have signs telling people they have to wear pants to enter McDonald's! On each return to the U.S. part of me wants people to have enough pride, dignity, or self-respect to dress like they give a damn about life. This is not to say that people shouldn't dress in a way that helps them express themselves, please do. Conscious self-expression, an outward sign that you have an inner awareness about yourself is wonderful. White socks and shorts, sweatpants and "comfortable clothes," sloppiness of any sort at the airport, main square, *riva*, or anywhere public, just suggests you are not only unaware, you're probably comatose.

CHAPTER 17

The Wonderful World of Zetdom

Alright, aside from the abundance of advice, the wind, and wearing *papuče*, I had adapted, acclimated to life in Croatia, to life in Split. Having coffee, going to the sea, talking to the neighbors, shaking my head and nodding when I didn't understand what some stranger was saying to me. I was moving through the motions, flowing, swimming in the new culture. I learned the local trails, the best beaches around, the back way to the center passing the old men playing *balota*, traversing through Radunica, or cutting down the back of Koteks, the shopping center built for the future that wasn't. I also learned our *kvart*, the hood. I could navigate the paths between the housing blocks from Vida's to the *Pazar*. I was finally in a state of recognition from the sellers in the neighboring stores and kiosks. The city had become familiar, but beyond the surface of geographical orientation something else was at work.

It turns out that I had joined a club that I didn't even know existed until I joined. I was and am a *splitski zet*, which kind of sounds like a race of alien from *Star Trek: The Next Generation* (we are the *Zet*), but actually it means I am married to a woman from Split. I've learned that along with sounding like something Sci-Fi, this phrase translates horribly because in English we have no other way of saying *I am married to a woman from Split* other than saying *I am married to a woman from Split*. So, there is no English equivalent to the phrase *splitski zet*. And back in the States, if I called my wife a daughter-in-law of Tulsa, people would have absolutely no idea what I was talking about. They would think my wife had received some honorary title, bestowed on her by the mayor and the city council at a ceremony involving flowers, a sash, and maybe even a parade. The idea that one's attachment to their homeland is transferable to their spouse is a strange concept to Americans. In the U.S., you don't have to marry-in to become an American (of course *you can*), but most of us come from someone who, at some point, just showed up and stayed.

What I was now feeling in Split was a deepening relationship between myself and the city, through the holy bonds of matrimony (not really HOLY since we just had a civil ceremony, but whatevs) I had become inextricably tethered to Split. I had gained a wife, a family, in-laws, and a city. Ever since I'd left home at 19, living in New Orleans, Montreal and Istanbul, I never felt as at home as in Split. Despite all of the initial awkwardness between our cultural differences I felt like I was home. I know, it's a little hard to understand (does it sound a little too much like a magic? Yes? Good!).

By having the label of *zet,* a term of inclusion in what is ultimately a bounded and limited community, I am invited (*maybe* even expected?) to experience the love for the hometown or homeland as much as my family from there. And it works. Split is important to me because it is important to my wife. It is where I proposed to her. It is where my daughter was born. And most of all, it is where I truly fell in love with her. Until I saw her in Split, amid the memories and familiarity that surround her here, I didn't really know her. Now, partly because of the city's own timelessness, but more from the effects of being a *zet,* I feel as if I am a part of this city and those memories.

The world of *zetdom* emphasizes the importance Vana, Vida, family, neighbors, and fellow residents place on where they are from. It is incomparable to our relationship with place in America.[7] The attachment people have for the place they are from in Croatia cannot be compared to anything I have felt in the U.S.[8] If you ask someone where they are from, she will either tell you where her family is from, or she will look frustrated and say something like: "Well, I grew up in Zagreb, but my

---

7 Unless you're from Pittsburgh, people from Pittsburgh are OBSESSED with being from Pittsburgh. Of course, Pittsburgh also has an absurdly high number of Croatians and people with Croat ancestry so…
8 Not even Pittsburgh!

father is from Dalmatia and my mother is from Zagorje, so… but I–I grew up in Zagreb." It is not uncommon for a friend to refer to his village on some island in Dalmatia that he and his parents have never ever even lived in, but that's where his family is "from," so it's "his village." I even have a friend from Osijek whose father traced his heritage back 400 years in Slavonia, but to him this explained why he often felt like an outsider because before those 400 years his family had lived in Herzegovina!

Can you imagine if we tried this in the U.S.? I'm from Oklahoma, but really I'm from Pennsylvania and Arkansas, via Georgia, via Hamburg, Prussia and also Derry, Ireland when all of Ireland was in the U.K. Because my great-great-grandfather came over on the boat from Hamburg, and my paternal grandfather from Derry, via Belfast in 1911!

While Americans are physically separated from our homelands and in the Croatian sense there is a spiritual separation as well, we are often mentally obsessed with them. Americans are fascinated with the idea of a return to the land of their great-great-grandparents, even if just for a summer vacation. Even for those of us who don't manage to traverse the skies for Europe, the longing for that other shore exists within us. This is especially evident in the *Diaspora* communities that dot the American landscape. Irish, Italians, Croats, Serbs, Latvians, Poles, all of us celebrate the lands that once made our ancestors refugees (I'm sure so do non-European Americans from Central or South America, Vietnam, the Philippines, China or Japan who want to glimpse their past homelands.) Beneath the buzz of life in America exists an idea tugging at the back of our consciousness. Deep down, there is, in every American, the half-hearted hope that we will one day return. While the constraints of finance, travel and language dampen the likelihood of an ancestral homecoming, we can still feel ourselves grasping for it. So we grab onto things like Irish Parades, St. Patrick's Day, German-American Day (Oktoberfest in Oklahoma?).

My membership in the *zet* club was helping ease this longing for a homeland, even if it was by proxy or substitution. My feelings toward Split were more visceral since the city was also the birthplace of my daughter. Pretend as I might that *zetdom* was a bonding agent between me and this seaside town, the bond would be real for Sara. So, now that I was in the club, Split's affection for Split was rubbing off on me. All the other towns and cities I had lived in felt like acquaintances, while Split, she felt like family.

And that's why we then moved to Zagreb in September? No. We moved to Zagreb for the same reason every *Splićan* moves to Zagreb: work and opportunity. *Splićani* in Zagreb, are like exiles. They long to return to Split, to live and work in the city of their dreams and yet they are forced to live abroad in Zagreb (even if abroad is in the same country and only four hours away by car). Like the multitudes before us, we loaded up the car with our meager belongings and emigrated to Zagreb.

★ **ZAGREB**

CHAPTER 18

Zagreb

Zagreb was a sort of fantasy. With it's endless winter gray, crumbling facades and socialist constructed periphery, Zagreb was everything I imagined when I imagined communism. In Split, the sea and living Roman remains of Diocletian's Palace are too distracting to think of single party rule, red stars, sickles and hammers, and well, tanks. Of course you don't see any of that in Zagreb nowadays, but these were mere props on the set of the Zagreb stage. Once in Zagreb, I finally had the feeling I was in Europe, Central and Eastern Europe. Here, history could happen.

In the gray murk of the winter months, the city is awash with indistinct visions. Like a somnambulant's haven, Zagreb is both spooky and familiar as one can only experience in a reoccurring dream. Where there was no there, there, in the abundant towns of the American Midwest, Zagreb has something, a feeling, a story, around every corner. Vrbik's rockets tell the tale of a failed future, of aspirations pinned on the hopes of a socialist cosmonaut hurtling through the cosmos.

In shrouds of fog, the city's other socialist relics disappear, only to reappear through the mist like the ruins of a fallen temple from some forgotten past, in some a hidden land. The cafe lights are brighter amid the gloom, like beacons to the gray ghosts that live in each of us. At night there lurk an endless amount of questions in each covered walk and behind each crumbling facade. The backdrops of rust and ruination invite an untold number of stories that the shiny and new can never tell. What's more, is the way these are just the background for the life that pulses through these city streets. The clatter of trams, phosphorescent pops on their lines, pedestrians, foot traffic, people, faces passing by, all of this tells you that you are somewhere even when you are headed to nowhere in particular.

Recalling, the geography of every midwestern American city: they all have a generic business district, houses, highways, parking lots, shopping malls, suburbs. They have very little mystery. The streets are barren, save for the lives of passing cars. The seasons come and go with little impact on how we live our lives.

With spring in Zagreb your sleepwalking ends, you awaken and the indistinct becomes lucid, the shadows creep back to their nests and Zagreb bursts with life, in the cafes. *Ah the cafe-culture I've heard so much about in Paris…is…here…in Zagreb?*

You're damn right. Once it's warm, there is nowhere else to be, but on the shaded terrace of one of the 1,901 cafes in the city. Oh, but how utterly, wonderfully different this is from my hometown, where to sit on a terrace in summer means to melt in the 104° F heat or to have the furnace-like air blow dust and dirt into your beverage. Coffee can never be coffee in the air-conditioning and everything in Oklahoma is air-conditioned.

In summer, like a wilting flower, drying in the heat, the city dies. Again it fills with ghosts, as all of the living make to the coast. From July to September Zagreb is barren of all the hassle it brings in the other months: lines, traffic, impossible-to-find parking spaces. It is a capital city in miniature. The rhythm of the city falters, shrinking to but the beating heart in the city center. Even empty, the city offers you a different view: a small-town feel in a metropolis.

As autumn embarks the city returns to life, filling as the leaves are falling. Waiters put out heaters in a small attempt to extend the outside sitting season. Chestnuts roast on carts, whose peddlers burn a fuel with an acrid smell that is distinct across all of Southeastern Europe. It and cigarette smoke are like the Balkan's perfume, it's a scent that you can smell in Zagreb, Belgrade, first brought to the touch of my nose on those November days in Istanbul. To compare Zagreb and Istanbul is for the most part impossible, but there are traits that both cities share. Each has a certain sadness contained in the exposed brick and mortar of its older buildings. A cloak of melancholy that beseeches you to look at what the city once was and could have been, rather than to focus on what it is not and never will be. And in the autumn mornings and twilight just before dark the air permeates with a haze that seems to somehow hide the present, but reveal the past. It's as if breathing in the chilly fall air, you are actually no longer breathing in the now, but rather breathing in the millennia of memories that inhabit everything around you.

CHAPTER 19

Finding an Apartment

In New York or San Francisco apartment hunting is a way of life. My friends that live in both cities are always on the lookout for an apartment with lower rent, better rent control, a little bit more space or slightly closer to this or that metro or BART stop. They live like urban nomads and have become experts on renters' rights, and square footage, weary of slumlords. They are connoisseurs of the rental market, able to spot a fine sauvignon at great price and avoid that overpriced merlot.

In Zagreb, there is no rental market. There pretends to be one, but there isn't. When we decided to move, our plan was to drive up to Zagreb from Split, leaving our beloved Sara at home with her grandma and aunt, and spend the day finding an apartment. We had one day. We enlisted the help of a rental agency, spoke with them three times prior to our trip, explaining each time what we were looking for: a two-bedroom apartment in Trešnjevka or Trnje. On the fateful day we called the agency a fourth time, they acted like they had never heard of us, told us it was OK, they would find something and call us back. It was the last time we ever heard from those shitheads.

We had two other options and a third one called us on the way, because my wife had placed an ad on an online message board. The first apartment we couldn't see because the occupants didn't answer the landlord's phone call and the landlord was out of town, even though we had spoken earlier in the week to confirm that we were coming on that Saturday to look at the apartment. Compared to the industrialized machine of house flipping, property investment and slumlordism that characterizes the housing and rental market all over the U.S., Croatia's rental and housing market is like comparing a tricycle to a 21-speed mountain bike. No one riding it seems concerned with how far they will get or if they will even get there.

The other problem with renting a place is not just finding someone who might actually show you the place that's advertised for rent, but also finding a place with decent furniture. See, renting in Croatia is not an investment. It's an afterthought. Usually someone just ends up owning an extra apartment. Some aunt dies or something and well, you can't sell it because it's been in the family for 400 years or something, so the best thing to do is rent it, but you also can't get rid of the furniture because that's also been in the family for the last 60 years, and well by golly they just don't make couches like they used to back in Yugoslavia. So the best thing to do is leave it as it is, with all the cluttered knick-knacks, old books and mismatched furniture sets, gathered over time, and rent it.

Apartment hunting with furnished apartments is an entirely new experience for a guy from Oklahoma. In the U.S., our apartments are completely empty. Maybe an errant hanger dangles in the closet, but generally speaking American apartments are like blank canvases ready for you to fill with your own vision of hearth and home.

On our search in Zagreb some of the flats looked forlorn, like the back room of an antique shop or my grandfather's garage. Others still felt so lived in that looking at them felt like trespassing. By noon, the one apartment we were actually able to see we crossed off our list just by the ghosts that emerged from the closets. Personal effects: children's toys, a pair of heels, a rumpled shirt. Each item left in a disarray that suggested an unhappy story, some form of flight or eviction. I knew we couldn't live among such visceral forms of someone else's unfortunate memories.

Nearing the end of the day we went to see the apartment that responded to Vana's own ad. Things started well because we met the actual owner and his wife in a cafe near the apartment. The neighborhood was exactly where we wanted it to be, in Trnje, but closer to Trešnjevka, in Vrbik. And the apartment: even better. It had been a business, and so it looked more like a law firm than a home, but the landlord was willing to buy a new couch, new bed, and best of all the place already had a huge desk, just perfect for working on my dissertation. Sold.

But despite the rare excellence of our apartment, it was still furnished with furniture that wasn't ours. In the U.S. when I moved around, my parents used my rented apartment to store their old furniture. The result was that each flat, house, hovel and shanty that I ever rented actually felt more like home than home. While my parents modernized their living room, I filled mine up with the same furniture I had been raised with. Years after moving out I continued to live with the well-known fabric and brown tones of the couch, lamp and table set that permeated my earliest childhood memories. My apartment was so familiar it was like I lived with inanimate siblings.[9] And even when you don't have your childhood furniture (I recommend sleeping in a race car bed well into your 20s), furnishing your apartment helps make it your home. You get to pick out that chair and that bookshelf. And one of the best ways to do this is with the GARAGE SALE!

Now, my only experience with garage sales in Croatia is Vida's reaction to seeing one on *Everybody Loves Raymond*. I was sitting in the kitchen eating a snack when she started yelling for me to come into the living room. She pointed in disbelief at the TV, exclaiming: *They are selling their furniture in*

---

9 Excluding, of course, my apartments in Montreal, New Orleans and Istanbul.

front of their house. Just like that! Yes, that is a garage sale. Is something lost in translation? (Probably.)

Why is it that Americans have no problem piling their old, unwanted wares on their lawn and selling them? The garage sale is a suburban institution. People spend their entire Saturdays cruising through neighborhoods looking for garage sales. Corners become crowded with signs announcing this sale here or that sale there. We even have urban legends about an art collector finding a *Picasso* for cheap in the back of some old garage, or the comic collector spying an *Amazing Fantasy No. 15* among a pile of otherwise worthless comics. True or not, the garage sale is a bargain hunter's paradise. They are also a great way to either furnish or unfurnish your apartment.

Now you might be saying: *Cody? C-bone, how you can complain about used furniture in your apartment and then GO AND BUY a BUNCH of USED FURNITURE AT A GARAGE SALE!?! I MEAN COME ON!*

Good point, but purchasing used furniture and inheriting it temporarily from anonymous owners involves an important distinction. When you hunt down that lava lamp at the garage sale you are empowered. YOU found that used lava lamp and the minute you purchase it YOU will remember it as the boss-awesome lava lamp that YOU found and got for a great price. This is very different from renting an apartment and seeing a sad, sagging armchair that some odd stranger might have had sex on or even died in. Your garage-sale-purchased lava lamp is a symbol of individual initiative and choice. It is rock-n-roll. The other is imposed on you. It is Muzak on a really long elevator ride.

So why do Croatians seem to cling to their used wardrobes and credenzas? The only time I see used furniture is on that big trash day or at Zagreb's super flea market, Hrelić. Is there a public shame with selling used goods? Or buying them? Is this why *njuškalo,* the local craigslist, flourishes? You can buy and sell used goods in the privacy of your own home. One friend suggested that the lack of garage sales could come from the power of social connections. If you have something you don't want, then you should give it to a friend, rather than try selling it to a stranger (I'm imagining that the day the secret gift cupboard is empty you then give the gift cupboard to a friend). Or is all this a result from the fact that, though there is a surplus of furniture in Croatia, there is a dearth of garages?

Whatever the reason, we lucked out. Our new Zagreb apartment was nice, newish and in the best neighborhood in all of Zagreb. **VRBIK 4 LIFE BITCHES.** So, a week later I packed the car with all of our stuff and drove up to Zagreb while Vana and Sara flew in that afternoon.

CHAPTER 20

Why My Punica is Like a Drug Dealer

Once upon a time, a not so long time ago, I was an adult. I could cook real meals with fresh ingredients, I could entertain friends in a clean house. I usually woke up daily, made coffee, put on ironed dress-shirts and permanently pressed pants and then drove myself to work. I came home, made dinner and tidied up the house. In this forgotten time, I was a fully fledged, competent, functional adult.

Then I moved to Croatia and began living with Vida.

As I mentioned previously (in like the last five chapters), life in Split had become a veritable paradise, thanks in large part to *punica*. Shangri-La. Not only was I living near the azure beauty of the Adriatic Sea, but this strange, sage-like woman appeared to be occupied with anticipating all of my eating needs. I would wake in the morning, stumble into the kitchen only to have a cup of coffee waiting for me on the table aside a chocolate *krafna*. I would go to the beach and come back to a home-cooked meal, flanked by at least two side dishes and a salad. I would be encouraged to drink wine with lunch and nap afterward while all of the dishes were washed and put away. Clothes too. All washed, hung on the line to dry, ironed and folded. Every day. EVER-Y DAY!

In America I never experienced anything like this from the time I was 10. Sure my mom cooked dinner most nights, but it was never done with an intense sense of urgency as when *punica* made lunch. It was just dinner. My mom washed my clothes, but again, once I came back from college, or on summer break, this was considered my responsibility. If I wanted to smell like a hobo and wear dirty clothes, that was both my prerogative and my problem. Eventually, as I grew older all of the essential elements of living, food, washing, hygiene and domestic cleanliness became my responsibility. No one was going to pick up after me, nor were they expected to. Maybe it's my family's stern Protestantism or just a lack of concern about my well-being in general, but even before I turned 18, the older generation (mothers, fathers, grandmothers included) never catered to my or my sister's needs with such doting attentiveness. One of the last times I went home (and this is after living in Istanbul, Croatia, and Kansas), I was told by my father, upon arrival, that, we probably had some bologna we could make sandwiches with for dinner, and if I wanted something else I could go to the store and get it myself!

Needless to say, the contrast between my family's austere policy of self-reliance and my *punica's* indulgence was huge.

Little did I know, but these first feelings of euphoria were just the novice's rush. As time drifted on I began to notice that *punica* did not actually seem all that concerned with my comfort or with my gratitude. I would say thank you each time she gave me coffee, cooked me lunch, handed me a stack of folded clothes and she would swipe her hand at me as if she was literally knocking my uttered *"Hvala"* out of the air. It finally dawned on me that *punica* wasn't serving me in order to obtain my gratitude. Driving her was not hospitable kindness, but rather a kind of stubborn duty guided by the belief that without her cooking and cleaning we would all die of starvation in a state of extreme filth!

Eventually, I began to resist. I suggested to her that *maaaybe I could cook lunch*? She replied:

"Ma daj! Can you cook soup?"

"I think so?" I said.

And that was that. My slight uncertainty, that little hiccup of hesitation was enough to convince her that her assumptions were right. Without her to cook lunch we would starve. I imagined a golden banner draped above the kitchen, reading:

**HE WHO CANNOT COOK SOUP,
CANNOT COOK LUNCH.**

I even tried to do my own laundry, once. Again I was deterred and told I wouldn't know how. As it turned out the washing machine was in German, so she was basically right. But I think her words were less about me not understanding what *Schoneaschgang* meant and more about my lacking the artistry necessary for the alchemy of laundering.

SO FAR THE SCORE WAS:
PUNICA: 2 ME: 0

More importantly, nothing I said or did could change *punica's* mind: without her I would be as helpless as I was the day I was born.

Then came that wonderful, glorious day we moved to Zagreb. I drove up to the capital from Split, grooving to tunes and feeling wonderfully, fully free. And just like a true addict, I insisted that I didn't have a problem. Mentally I ranted about how once we were on our own things (whatever they were) would go back to normal, I would cook and clean just like I had once done in that far and distant past. With clenched determination I vowed: I WILL BE ME AGAIN!

The first day was fine. We had moved and were tired so we just ordered a pizza. The pizza fixed us for the night and the next day. But the second night we caved and had some *ćevapi*.

And by the third night I knew it was hopeless. While under the sway of *punica* my muscles of responsibility and self-sufficiency had atrophied. I was strung out. The dust and dirty clothes began to gather in the house, used bottles and newspapers piled up, paper towels replaced plates, and each afternoon the kitchen table just stood there food-less, barren, a desolate reminder of our desperate situation.

The horror of my situation hit me. Looking around the messy apartment, fighting my pangs of hunger I thought: *NOOOOOOOOO! She was right! Without her I will starve and die in a state of filth.* The house was a disaster and I was hungry. My independence, my self-reliance, my old-self, were now just an illusion. Just images I clung to in a fit of self-delusion. There was no denying it now. I was addicted to *punica's* heavy hand of hospitality!

And just like junkies craving another fix, we pleaded for her to come up to Zagreb, begged her to stay with us. And we rejoiced when she came, overcome with the sweet relief of seeing lunch cooling on the table. When my mother-in-law stayed with us, there was a warm comfort in the air. It was like we were high.

Like a drug dealer pushes his dope to get you hooked, *punica* pushes her hospitality to make you as dependent as she imagines you already are. It is a self-fulfilling prophecy. You may fight back, you may tell yourself that you don't have a problem, that you can quit anytime, and that she's just being nice, but by that point it's already too late. She's got you in her power. If you ever had any kind of self-reliance, well buddy, it's long gone. But, the first step to overcoming your problem is admitting you have one. So say it with me: My name is Cody and I'm addicted to *punica*.

And that is just how she wants it.

CHAPTER 21

Drinking

After moving to Zagreb things got more social. As Zagreb is a city of Croatian immigrants, from Slavonia, Dalmatia, Zagorje, and Istria, the mortar in the circle of friends isn't as set as it is in places where people have had the same friends for decades. In other words, Vana's Zagreb social circle was more inclusive and less exclusive than its Dalmatian equivalent. Also, I was here to do research and so I actually began branching out and finding my own contacts and connections. I hung around the political science faculty, attending a few classes, and started befriending Zagreb's eclectic group of expats.

On most occasions if I was out with someone we drank coffee, but other times we went out drinking, like drinking, drinking. And if there is one thing Croatians love that comes close to coffee, it's alcohol. This probably helps explain why Croatians, and well, everyone else all over Southeastern Europe makes booze out of everything. And I mean everything: cherries, plums, grapes, walnuts, honey, quince (I don't even know what that is) ROSES, yes ROSES! and grass,[10] it all goes into *rakija*. But, all this shouldn't leave the impression that Croatians are a bunch of drunkards. As I went out with my wife's friends or my own acquaintances, I saw that drinking in Croatia is treated with a certain reverence and elegance that is usually lacking in the U.S.

In America the days of *Mad Men*, where beautiful, well-dressed people stoically drink martinis are gone. Elegant drinking has been replaced with the beer bong and beer pong. Nothing spells elegance like four feet of plastic tubing and a funnel that lets you drink four beers in three seconds! Or how about beer pong? All over the U.S. undergrads drink according to whether or not they can toss a plastic ball into a plastic cup. Nor does Croatia seem to have drinks for people who don't like to drink, like the chocolate-flavored Mudslide, fruit-flavored 'tinis, or strawberry-kiwi daiquiris, or the dreadful candy-rainbow flavors of Mad Dog 20/20. I've never even seen a daiquiri or any other fruity drink in Croatia. Nope, in Croatia if you wanna drink, well pardner you better be able ta drink. That liquor made from roses only tastes like roses at the beginning, as it slides onto the back of your tongue and slips down your throat it then feels like the cleansing burn of a thousand suns! It's more like rose-flavored rocket fuel (and it's almost always

---

10 Dear Croatians, I understand that *travarica* is not made straight from grass, but rather from herbs, that could just as easily be confused as grass. In any case, it sounds funnier to say grass.

homemade). The one thing the kids do is mix Coca-Cola with wine to create what they call a *bambus*, but it's taste doesn't come close to any of the sweet alcohol-suppressing concoctions that flood college bars and high school parties. Even the beer is *FORTE!* The dribble-piss water of Keystone Light and Milwaukee's Best are not to be found. Here, it is important that you taste and experience the alcohol. Not, slurp down something that's closer to Skittles or a chocolate sundae just in order to get drunk.

The respect for drinking is so strong and steeped in such ritualisms that a lot of alcohol is treated with the same care and reverence as if it had incredible medicinal properties, because well…a lot of people believe it is medicine. Especially *rakija*. In most houses (maybe next to the secret cupboard of gifts) exists a cabinet filled with various, often unlabeled bottles. Floating within the opaque liquid inside are gestating leaves and herbs, clipped from various plants that give the spirit its medicinal qualities. According to local lore, it's healthy to drink a shot of *rakija* every morning in the winter as it warms you up and… somehow it is *equally* important to drink a shot of *rakija* in the summer as it cools you down. I've also been told that if you have a fever you can rub *rakija* all over yourself as a means of lowering your temperature.

On that early trip to Croatia when I was beset with a horrible cold, the neighbor doctor came and examined me and then gave me a bag of lemons and a bottle of *travarica* (grass *rakija*)! And actually, drinking it (plus some cold medicine) made me feel much better.

Going out and drinking in Croatia is treated with the same lackadaisical, easygoingness that characterizes much of the country. There is never a hurry. In the long-lost days of my youth there always seemed to be a rush to get drunk (hence the beer bong). It was as if the fun couldn't start until we reached that point where the world spun and our self-conscious diffidence collapsed. So we choked back the vodka, tequila, or rum, chasing it with orange juice, apple juice or Coke just so we could hurry up and reach the edge of oblivion, all perched, and ready to leap off. This was also, almost always, done in the shadows, away from the prying eyes of the law. The high drinking age of 21 and the still-present desire to get drunk from the first rustling of adolescence, forced us to drink like criminals, well into our college careers, we had to find those tucked-away places where we could imbibe without being observed. Another reason to rush, *Quick! Get drunk before we're found out.* But then the drinking is less about the drinking and more about the law. And, I suppose the ever-present prospect of drunken, awkward sex.

Probably the biggest difference between drinking in the U.S. and in Croatia is that you can drink in cafes. While in America you usually have to go to the bar. Once I was old enough to emerge from the secret apartments, party houses, and catacombs of underage drinking, I found that most American bars are depressing, especially bars in my home state, Oklahoma. Dark and dingy you can feel the years of spilt beer soaked into the ratty carpet, surrounded by thick coats of cigarette smoke painted across the wood-paneled walls. Usually there is a horrible display of taxidermy somewhere on the wall, collecting dust and cobwebs above you, deer, duck, fish and in New Orleans a few mummies. You can also feel the drunken desperation of the people who have come before you. The bar is much different than the cafe. Bars are scenes of drunken, physical dalliances, where inhibitions are suppressed only with copious amounts of alcohol. Or it is a place to kill time. Where you drink after work only as a means to more easily stand on the bridge between today and tomorrow. My memories of bars are like blurry photographs captured in the naked light of a neon sign. They are staggered, stinking, and sloshy.

Cafes, on the other hand, are clean and well-lighted. I learned that sitting on the terrace of a Zagreb cafe in the spring, summer, or early fall can be an experience filled with Zen-like contentment. With the sights and sounds of the city surrounding you, the night air still and endless, you feel elated with life. Everything is charming: your company, the bored waiters, the passersby. Rather than being shut away from the world in neon hues, you are out in the world, a part of its harmonious ambience. Surrounding you is a diverse clientele that demands you behave. Your drinking has to be elegant. Since an older couple is talking over tea next to you, a group of women are having coffee beside you, there is no place for the sloppy drunk (that place is across the street in the park). No place for loud chanting and body shots. No whoo-girls. No ping-pong balls. This is not a place to get drunk. It is a place to converse over drinks, or, if you are by yourself it is a place to sit and just BE, a place to reflect on passing trams and the drip-like passage of time.

In Zagreb (and Croatia), time is never forced on you. For some reason the culture seems to put less emphasis on getting to the end of the line and more emphasis on the journey there. Have a drink, have another, get drunk, but take your time. Like most things in Croatia, no one is ever in a hurry, even when fun is involved. During those early days and months in Zagreb, the pace of drinking and being out made me feel like I was living my life in a novel, a piece of literature, rather than trying to imitate an MTV reality show.

CHAPTER 22

Party Breaking

Now, Croatians may not be in a rush to DESTINATION: FUN, but the fare for the ride is a one-way ticket. Once you arrive at FUN, you have to stay. Not so in America, we honestly have no problem ending the fun. It's 2 a.m.: the party is jumpin', the music bumpin' and everyone is just having a great time, but *I gotta go home. You know I got a…thing…in the morning. Just let me pay for my own drinks and c'ya. Bye-bye.* No one blinks. You disappear into the night like the fading bass from a passing car. You're just an afterthought. It is the least bit of concern for everyone else who disembarked at the stop for FUN. Or, if we are actually hosting the good time, we will even suggest *strongly* that you (and everyone else) leave our party so we can go to bed. *It's getting late. YAAAWN! And I've got a big…um…in the morning. So…*

Croatians on the other hand hate, I mean hate, to end a good time. Even when this good time turns out to be a birthday party… for. a. two-year-old, attended. by. other. two-year-olds. Now, I kind of knew that Croatian evenings out can last until dawn, but this was when, you know, we were out with grown-ups, not toddlers. Well, one foggy December night I was introduced into the realities of Croatian hospitality when we took our then one-and-a-half-year-old daughter to a birthday party for one of Vana's coworker's kids out in Novi Zagreb. The party started at 5 p.m., and being Croatian we showed up at 6 p.m. and left much, much later.

In Croatia, there is never an excuse good enough or strong enough to peel yourself away from the fun (even your toddler's bedtime, which in the U.S. is THE excuse for everything). There are probably lots of reasons why there is such a big difference between Croatian F-U-N and American fun. But I think a lot has to do with social expectations. In Croatia, no one wants to be the "party breaker." *A what?* You ask. *Right.* This is a term Croatians have invented, in English!, that doesn't even exist in the American lexicon. Basically the party breaker is as follows:

party breaker \\'pär-tē\ \'brā-kər\: the person who first leaves a night out, a gathering of people, a party, or any other good time and by leaving thereby ruins the party and everyone else's good time.

The first to leave is the party breaker. It's like the party is in some happy state of equilibrium, and the first to move will alter the stability, creating an exodus of partygoers streaming into the street. So you, and everyone else, are basically held captive by each other (and by fun). You just can't leave, even if you wanted to. If you leave, well buddy, YOU, and you alone, will be responsible for ending everyone's good time (way to go JERK!).

So back at the toddler birthday party, the hours creep by and before we know it, it's 9 p.m. and I suggest to Vana:

"Hey it's late we should get Sara home."

And then she's all like: "No, no we can't be the first ones to leave." And I'm like:

"Saaaaay what?" And so we wait. And wait. And this goes on and on. In fact, the later it gets the more I'm constantly looking at my watch, trying to get Vana's attention and looking for a way to escape the fun. Here's a picture:

You can't escape, it's like a Chinese finger trap. The more you struggle to get out, the more you're sucked in. In most cases, the host can sense that you want to flee, and so she (or he) entices you with more to eat, more to drink, all things that will keep the gears of fun well-lubricated and grinding. And this is also ironic because the host might actually also want you to leave, but there is no greater sin than for the host to be the party breaker. We're talking Judas here. There have even been occasions when some people offer to just let us spend the night.

The real truth about party breaking is that it's a lot like hostage-taking. Everyone is hostage to the fun! No one leaves! Playing the party hostage game is wrapped up in the responsibilities of friendship and hospitality. Its like a self-perpetual motion machine: the host, hosts the party and it's then the friends' responsibility not to break it, while the friends went to all the trouble of coming to the party, so the host has to be sure the party doesn't break. The party can go on into perpetuity (or at least until the sun comes up, not dawns, but up, like 8 a.m.).

Parties in Croatia are much more um…fun, than in America? The expectations are much, much higher. I asked a Croatian friend who studied in Chicago what the parties were like. After laughing for five minutes, he said something to the effect that a "party" in Chicago involved a cheese platter, everyone bringing some food and their own drinks, talking nicely, showing up at 8 p.m. and leaving before midnight. Those massive house parties you see in the movies mostly died with the 1980s and John Hughes. Now they can only be spotted, rarely, at fraternities and sororities.

And this isn't some young people versus old people issue. Croatians enjoy a good time well into their twilight years. One night our 70-year-old Vida stayed out until 4 a.m. with her septuagenarian friends, dancing at a wedding. What's more is that as the night goes on, the hosting never falters. Like a watchful member of the party-police, the host is always aware of how empty your glass is, and is there to replenish it. The fun must go on!

A few weeks after the two-year-old's birthday party, which we eventually left around 10:30 p.m., because all the kids simultaneously had a breakdown, Vana and I attended a New Year's Party (leaving Sara with Vida). It started at 10 p.m. and went until dawn and as the early morning approached, our hosts, like stewards and stewardesses on a transatlantic flight, shifted to a small breakfast service, providing us with Earl Grey tea and light morsels in the place of *rakija*, beer, and *pelinkovac*.

By then, with the gray light of dawn slipping through the curtains, the party had broken. But no one was the breaker, instead it was the resumption of life's natural volatility that carried us home. The day had brought change, and change is inevitable. Stasis cannot last forever, no matter how hard we try. Entropy endures.

Given all the expectations, responsibilities, and reciprocity involved in having a good time in Croatia, it's no wonder that having this kind of a good time is socially acceptable. For us in the U.S., staying out all night is something only "wild" teenagers should do. For people in their mid-30s and up, staying out all night is seen as irresponsible and something the "town fathers" certainly frown upon. Whereas in Croatia it means you are a good friend, a good host, or both. The guilt-ridden cab ride through the foggy dawn doesn't exist. I find that in those early-morning moments, after a fun evening, amid the bad breath and stale smell of cigarettes, I become more reflective, thinking ever-so-lightly on the passing night, and how great it is to have such exhausting fun with friends. In those moments, I feel we could stay young forever.

CHAPTER 23

Splitting the Ticket

Back when Vana lived in Oklahoma, there was one other Croatian in our college town. He and his wife invited us to have dinner with them. This was the first time I had any kind of meal with a Croatian other than Vana.

We went to Applebee's. Applebee's is famous for serving mediocre food with mediocre alcohol. Nothing says *meh*, like overcooked, rubbery ribblets (a word Applebee's invented) and cold 3.2 beer. In rural Oklahoma, our Croatian friend found Applebee's to be the closest thing to civilization north of I-44. So much so, that he seemed to order half of the menu. Sides of french fries, starters of fried onions and buffalo wings clogged our table, like the grease clogging the other patrons' arteries. Drinks, dinner and dessert, it all came our away.

And this annoyed me. I had been duped into this "type" of situation before. You go out to eat with someone and they order a bunch of "shared" appetizers and then you end up paying for half of it. I didn't want honey-glazed buffalo wings with a side of honey mustard. I didn't really want the Applebee's version of guacamole. What I wanted was to order my hamburger and beer, eat and drink, and then pay my $11.54 share of the bill, plus tip (that's right, I wasn't even planning on paying for Vana's meal!). A quarter into our Croat buddy's ordering and the bill had well exceeded my budget. So, rather than enjoy in the near infinite amount of offerings, I brooded and simmered in my own broth of thrifty resentment.

Then the bill came and to my surprise señor Croatian paid for EVERYTHING. My internal record scratched, the rhythm of my world was off, the music stopped: I was shocked. *What just happened?* I replayed the whole meal in my memory's reel to reel and chagrined. Now it all made sense. His insistence that I order more and more food, the sheer abandon with which he had the waitress bring us drinks. He wasn't try to trick me, he was...being a host. *Holy Crap!* I'd read about this kind of thing in books. You know, where someone invites you somewhere and treats YOU because THEY invited YOU. And I? I had just sat there nursing my beer and picking at my hamburger, fearing to eat any of the appetizers less I be damned to pay my share of the bill like Persephone was damned to spend three months a year in Hades.

After living awhile in Croatia, how we Americans insist on bill splitting began to seem so silly, so petty, that it could only really be described as miserly. Objectively speaking, Americans have more income than most Croatians, and yet when the bill comes we take out our smartphone calculators and divvy up the amount like a bunch of penny-pinching accountants. Here is an example of the extent to which this cultural tick permeates our society. After I turned 18, my own father and I used to split the bill over a breakfast. Shouldn't a son feel obliged to buy his father a meal now and then? And shouldn't a father buy his son breakfast? The answer is: yes. Why didn't we trade treating each other? I HAVE NO IDEA. Of course the irony is (and this is one of those core epiphanic ironies that once grasped is akin to crossing some kind of cultural Rubicon): We Americans, with more, spend like we have less, while Croatians with less, spend like they have more. *What?*

I think part of it concerns our strong desire to avoid, as much as humanly possible, being beholden to anyone. This kind of ambition explains why, when I first became familiar with the Croatian way of paying, I saw it just as some kind of score keeping. I HAVE to buy YOU a coffee because YOU bought ME a coffee; we HAVE to buy YOU dinner because YOU bought US a dinner; I bought YOU an ice cream so YOU BETTER buy ME one! And to a certain extent this is how it goes, but it's not as precise as my inner accountant imagined it. I've learned that the obligations created by paying for a friend's coffee are more nuanced than a clear *quid pro quo*. They are felt, not thought. It's like returning a catch rather than paying off a debt. You toss me the ball and wait to see if I toss if back. As the game gets going we no longer keep score. We come to enjoy playing just for the simple sake of playing (or paying).

CHAPTER 24

Wild West vs. Mild East

Growing up, I was aware that there was a war going on in Yugoslavia. The buzz words of Balkans, Sarajevo, Bosnian Serb, U.N. convoy, and ethnic cleansing were able to, at least partially, penetrate my adolescent brain (otherwise it was occupied with Pearl Jam, *Star Wars* and comic books). Even though I had no idea where Yugoslavia was, or what the war was about, and who was fighting it, I associated anything Yugoslav with Eastern Europe, and Eastern Europe with the Balkans, and the Balkans with barbaric violence.

My first trip to the region did little to assuage my initial impressions. Twelve years after the fighting ended and Sarajevo still looked ravaged. The pockmarked, bullet-riddled facades that still lined the main thoroughfares looked like acne on an otherwise pretty face. Mere shells of buildings haunted the periphery of the airport. The whole city seemed trapped in time, lodged in a limbo between the 1984 Winter Olympics and the 1990s' siege. Though the scene was what I had expected, seeing the intense legacy of the war, in the bas-relief of bombs and bullets, touchable, traceable scars all over the city was beyond anything I had ever experienced.

The bus ride through Western Bosnia and into Herzegovina was equally illuminating. In the hinterlands were the scorch marks around an abandoned mosque and the crumbled remains of a minaret. Parts of East Mostar, in the day's dying twilight were ghostly. Passing windows gazed into roofless rooms, so that the city seemed to be nothing but a battered, jagged silhouette, a passing shadow of death and destruction. Then we turned a corner and the headlights lit up a wall so utterly shot to hell that it was hard to understand how it could possibly still be standing. In those fleeting seconds each reminder of the war, each incomprehensible act of violence captured in the bus's headlights was like an insect specimen pinned to the board of my mind. Only, I didn't want to collect butterflies, I wanted to collect understanding.

In those early trips to Croatia, I eventually sought out and heard stories about the war from all of my immediate in-law family. Fortunately, there wasn't much to tell. But then, little bits would float to the surface, like the flotsam and jetsam still bobbing in the water above some long-sunken shipwreck. A story about a relative or old friend would suddenly veer into a story about the war. Talking about it is not something to take lightly. At dinner at a friend's house I would find out that the women sitting across from me had been in Vukovar during the Serb and JNA assault. Or I talked to some relatives about how some they had fled Osijek and came to live in Split when the fighting erupted there. Later I met a friend who had also fled Osijek, but in the other direction.

Partly because of my own interest in political violence, partly out of a desire to understand what happened to the people and the place I now loved and cared about, partly because I felt some sense of guilt for having been arguing endlessly about who could win in a fight, Wolverine or Spider-Man (I was a teenage comic geek) while my wife's country was burning, and finally because when in Croatia what else is there for an aspiring academic to do, but study the war, I embarked on a dissertation investigating the participation of Croatians in the early months of the war (don't worry, I'm not going to use this book as a forum to talk about my findings, coefficients or stinking Eigen values).

Thus my lucrative, U.S. government grant, the lifeblood that kept us afloat in Zagreb, was obtained so that I might travel around the country talking to war veterans. This is not an easy task. You can't well just show up and say: "Hi, I'm an American sponsored by the U.S. government and would like come talk to you about what are probably the most traumatic events in your life time." Needless to say, it took all kinds of contacts, machinations, connections, and goodwill to find people willing to talk to me. And on the way a strange thing happened. While I was steeped in the academic literature on conflict, the history of the war, and all the things I once associated with Croatia and the Balkans: violence, barbarism, brutality, I began to realize that actually life in Zagreb, and Croatia is generally much more peaceful, harmonious, and safer than life in America. Looking back across the Atlantic, I wasn't seeing an American bastion of peace and prosperity from the horribly brutal Balkans, but rather I was gazing at the wild west from the relatively mild east.

There were 506 murders in Chicago in 2012, just under that in New York, 386 in Detroit, 217 in Baltimore, 193 in New Orleans, and 46 in my hometown (an actual low, down from the high of 71 in 2009). When I lived in New Orleans, violence was just part of the description:

NEW ORLEANS! BEAUTIFULLY OLD, WONDERFULLY ORNATE, UNIQUE, HISTORICAL, ENTERTAINING... AND VIOLENT AS HELL.

Muggings around campus were common and at times even ingenuous, like when a four-door sedan was regularly pulling up beside a crowd of undergrads heading to the bar. Sticking out of the back passenger window was the barrel of a shotgun whose owner directed the college kids to toss their wallets, purses and cellphones into the front passenger seat. Working for a while as a delivery driver I carried a switchblade and a

Mag flashlight, in the vain hope that I could blind and then frantically stab any would-be assailant. Fortunately, I never had to put this ill-conceived plan into practice. The campus was often abuzz with rumors or stories of students falling prey to robbers and rapists. In one case a neighbor of mine in the student dorm, a trained Judo champion, was able to disarm and dislocate his attacker's elbow with one fluid Judo move. Why he was picked as a suitable victim and I wasn't, I'll never know. Maybe the criminal element in the Big Easy look for a challenge.

In the U.S., in towns like New Orleans, but in other less notoriously criminal places, the threat of violence is so present that we work caution into our routines. A lot of people even carry concealed handguns. Something as simple as walking down the street is complicated by the risk of robbery. In most cases if someone is walking toward you, or behind you, you cross the street and see if the other person follows. If they do, then your alarm bells ring and you look for help. Even just passing somebody on the street, you frequently prepare yourself for some altercation, some threat no matter how unlikely or arbitrary an attack might seem, it's better to be safe than sorry. In fact it's best to just drive and avoid any urban social interaction at all.

How do you explain this to a Croatian? You can't. Things here are so vastly different from the U.S. that it is often beyond your ability to convey what it is we are talking about. Coming home from a night out with a slight stumble and admittedly a bit shamed since I clearly broke the party, I encounter numerous people across my path, sometimes in packs of tracksuited dudes, sometimes as lone pedestrians, and never is there any indication that something might happen to me. Sure, I usually feel a slight hesitation, hackles begin to raise, but quickly fall as reality confronts instinct and we simply pass by, one good-natured human to another.

Over the year, as I meet with fellow expats this conversation always comes up. Why is it safer here in Croatia than in just about anywhere else in America? With the country's high unemployment rate and poverty we would expect everyone to be at each other's throat, robbing, raping, pillaging and again because, you know, Balkans! Of course none us ever come up with an adequate answer. The obvious answer is gun ownership, there are 93 guns in the U.S. per 100 people, but then again Serbia has the second highest gun ownership per capita and doesn't have the same problems as the U.S.

When the Sandy Hook Elementary School massacre occurred I was devastated. Not just by the senseless murder of elementary schoolchildren and their teachers, but by my country's response. Half the nation is yelling that the fact that a 20-year-old, mentally ill person could get easily get ahold of an assault rifle is somehow not part of the problem?[11] Then the

---

[11] See page 164.

most powerful lobby group in the U.S., submits its proposal to the legislature in the world's most powerful country and that proposal is to arm teachers so that they can shoot back in the event of another school massacre! Teachers in some schools in Arkansas have since been armed, and I'm thinking, did America move to the Balkans? This is what I would imagine people would have to do in war zones.

Then I walk my daughter to her *vrtić,* kindergarten. We are surrounded by other parents, hurrying their kids along, older students rushing to school. We are walking, catching eye contact, smiling, smirking in parental solidarity at each other when a kid yells: *neću!* We enter the school and I take Sara to her classroom, she is greeted by the teacher and enthusiastically by her friends. And I am amazed at how different life in Croatia is to what it was I imagined (remember, it's nothing like the *Bourne Identity*) and also how different life in America seems now than how I once imagined.

For the first time I understood why so much of the world is scared of America. The fact that the proposal to arm teachers is even accepted by a fraction of the society sounds crazy to anyone outside of the country. If a nation is willing to accept arming its teachers, but not accept that you know, there are

---

11 Just a note here that my sister has been very active in trying to get tougher legislation passed that would actually help restrict gun sales and the like. She was even mentioned, by name in a speech by President Obama for her efforts! She is one of the sane ones.

other things that could be done, like um...having less guns, or loving guns less, then sure it's easy to believe anything about that place. Conspiracy theories, CIA, toxic contrails, JFK, aliens, Area 51, why not? In some ways, America from the outside looks like an insane asylum that's being run by the inmates.

Over the course of my research I interviewed people all over Croatia. Sometimes in cafes, sometimes at their work, other times at their homes. To all of the participants, the war seemed like an aberration, something outside the normal course of life. It happened, it was violent, destructive and devastating, but then the calm returned. Meanwhile, in the U.S. it appears to be the exact opposite. For whatever the causes, or origins, violence endures. It may rise and fall, but there is a baseline that is now engrained into the very fabric of our daily lives. When it's part of the regular course of things, the news of school shootings has become so depressingly common that it is simply swallowed by the white noise background and it is hard to see how utterly awful all of it really is.

CHAPTER 25

Veze

Things were great! Here I was living in a capital of Europe, a place with stuff like a main square, a national theatre, and an archaeology museum (anyplace that has something called an archaeology museum already makes it cooler than anyplace that doesn't), trains, trams, and police sirens that sound like the ones in old movies. I was living the expat dream. We loved our neighborhood, it was like a verdant oasis of parks and trees just on the rim of the city's center. Sara loved her preschool and teachers. I was traveling around the country, doing the research I had always dreamed of doing. Life was grand.

But, we were left in a dilemma: do we stay or do we go? If life was so great, why leave? Well, my stipend was set to end in September and I had failed to attract any dissertation writing grants, which meant I would need a job. A job in Croatia, is actually one of the hardest things to find. I don't mean a job in academia or one suited to my interests, I mean a job. Period. Something that pays you a sufficient amount of money regularly, based on some kind of service you provide your employer. All the Croatian equivalents to the jobs I had in my life, the kinds of jobs all young people in the U.S. work at one point or another, bag boy at the grocery store, waiter at the Tex-Mex restaurant, coffee shop barista, delivery driver, bookstore-bookselling-guy, are difficult to find for Croatians, let alone a foreigner. Finding a full-time, steady, permanent job in Croatia, is like winning the lottery.

Looking around though, I felt like we had to try and stay in Croatia. If we went back to the States we would either live in Oklahoma, or more likely, in the event that I found a job as an Assistant Professor, we would live in a small town in Missouri or the like, while I taught at a small liberal arts college. I couldn't imagine taking Sara and Vana away from cultured Zagreb to the middle of nowhere middle America and saying with a sweeping hand: *Remember when we lived in a city with an archaeology museum? Well, this place has a Walmart and a Waffle House!*

So, how do you get a job in Croatia? A few ways. The most common way, or at least it seems to be the most common way, is through a connection of some sort. The all important *veze*. At its worst, this is just nepotism, at its least worst it is just like a reference or recommendation, often it is somewhere in between. A friend who graduated from the Faculty of Economics, told me that she tried really hard to get a job without any connections. She sent her CV to multiple companies and ministries and never received a reply. After that she asked her father if he knew anyone that could get her a job, he said he would see, and it turned out that his cousin or some relative worked in some bureaucracy somewhere dealing with finance or money and yes, he could hire her. She was hired and employed. Even with the right qualifications, you have to know someone to get your foot in the door. Even with the right qualifications, there is a chance that someone under-qualified with a better connection will be employed over you. I was told, in Croatia, this is just how it goes.

My problem was, I didn't have any connections. And connections aren't just needed to find employment, they are a daily fact of life. It is assumed you also need connections in order to navigate the bureaucracy. A professor at Kansas who was originally from Croatia, explained to me that as much as he would like to return, to come back and live in his hometown, he couldn't because he has been in the U.S. so long (20+ years) that all of his connections have withered away. This was the other consideration for us to stay, because for Vana, once we left, there was a good chance that we could never come back. The few connections she had, would be severed, cut, and then if we returned five, or 10 years later, we would be adrift in the society.

Aside from the fear of not being able to find work, the other frustrating part about *veze*, is that when you look at anyone who has a job, you wonder whether or not they secured that job from merit and expertise, or by exploiting a connection.

This breeds a social skepticism about anyone seen as successful. In the U.S., we are raised to believe that success is bred out of hard work. Of course advantage and privilege can help, but the belief that success in society is a product of your own effort and agency, what you do, rather than who you know, makes for a more optimistic people. The situation in Croatia induces a mistrust of success. This is something that is both understandable and unfortunate.

So, here we were ready to try to find a job. I met with everyone I knew and everyone my wife knew, or tried to, and asked them to help me find work. Of course I was leaning toward the academic side of things. I was a year out from completing my Ph.D. and most of my experience was involved in teaching. I had countless coffees, emailed numerous CVs to people, sat and discussed whom I should contact, where there might be a possibility for someone to find my services useful, and by September, I had nothing.

So far, life in Croatia had been life in a bubble, a U.S.-government-funded bubble. Now, as the funds in my account dwindled like the seconds ticking on a stopwatch. *Tick-tick-tick-tick-tick: CLICK!* I began to see the Croatia that most Croatians complained about. The Croatia that young people fled from, the Croatia that was suffering a brain drain, the Croatia that people associate with the Balkans: corrupt, nepotistic, and backward.

CHAPTER 26

The Dark Side

In America I was never really one for luxury cars. Not that I could ever afford one, but I never even dreamed of owning one. Never wanted to. Luxury car in the U.S. means a big, bulky SUV that annoys me more than it impresses me. Cadillac Escalades, Ford Excursions, Mercedes M-class, Cayenne, Humvees, I used to see all of them as a form of overcompensation for deficiencies in their drivers' character and personality. I was satisfied driving in my fuel-efficient, small, Toyota.

Yet, after living in Croatia for a while, I began to feel, for the first time the power of the Dark Side. Yes, there is a power emanating from Croatia's Holy Trinity of automobiles: The black Mercedes, black BMW and black Audi. While in America these cars may reflect prestige, they do not surround themselves with the same aura of enigmatic dominance as they do in Croatia. Here it is a strange force coming from these cars, both terrifying and alluring at the same time. A power that says beware and in the same breath, behold.

In front of my Zagreb apartment the black BMW parked crookedly across three parking spaces, abutting a spot for invalids, gave me the same feeling of apprehension as a proud black panther waiting to pounce. I knew the car was in the wrong. The car knew it was in the wrong. It knew, I knew, and it silently dared me, in a low and ominous growl, to do something about it. I didn't. I wouldn't. And no one will. Such is the power of the Dark Side.

If that same car was a Yugo (OK, it couldn't take up three spaces) or a Hyundai you might be tempted to say something. If you saw the driver, you might suggest that they not park like that, that they be respectful of invalids and other drivers. If you don't say anything, well at least with these lesser cars you *feel* like you *could*. They do not command the silent obedience as the mysterious Holy three.

Walking past the Mercedes sedan parked on the sidewalk I felt like Luke Skywalker at the end of *The Empire Strikes Back*. The car beckoned to me like Darth Vader. In a deep, sonorous voice it tempted me to join the Dark Side.

Just look at how this car breaks the rules with careless abandon, obstructing half the sidewalk with impunity. Its value is nearly 30 times what the average person in Croatia makes a year. To me it says the person driving this car is important. It is someone who may very well be above and beyond the law. In any case, the driver certainly lives out of the bounds of my mortal world.

In the U.S., rightly or wrongly, we still live under the impression that anyone who works hard enough will one day achieve success. I know several people, ranging from professors to friends and family that earn over one-hundred thousand dollars a year. As far as I know they have not achieved this position through favors, nepotism, corruption, or theft. They've simply been good at what they do and work hard when doing it. In America wealth is not yet considered a mystery. We do not have an innate distrust of success or its symbols.

In Croatia, however, no such illusion exists. Rather, wealth is shrouded in impossibility. I couldn't (and cannot) understand how someone in Croatia affords a BMW (Mercedes or Audi) and to me this was the source of these cars' mystique and power. Of course not everyone who drives a German luxury car is a scoundrel or a rogue. Yet, in Croatia these vehicles are more than mere symbols of success. They are symbols of someone who has defeated an impossible system, used the system, and dominated the system to their advantage while the rest of us just putter along in the distance. In a society where our lives appear to be increasingly subject to vindictive and arbitrary forces, unresponsive bureaucracy and indifferent politicians, the black BMW is a symbol of dark triumph.

What makes the gods divine is the unrevealed source of their power. We cannot fully understand why the gods are more powerful than us. Nor can we comprehend the full extent of that power. Though the origins of the Holy German automobiles' symbolic strength may be part of the very forces we hate (unfair advantage, better connections, crony capitalism), just like the gods we curse, the Promethean part of us would give anything to be one of the divine. If we only knew how. If only we knew the power of the Dark Side.

CHAPTER 27

Lines

Before moving to Croatia the longest lines I had ever seen were at Disney World in 1988. Actually, Disney World seemed to be nothing but lines, something Croatia and *"the happiest place on earth"* have in common. The difference being that most of the lines at Disney World end with you getting on a ride like *Pirates of the Caribbean* or *The Haunted Mansion*. Most lines in Croatia end with you stooping over to talk to someone through a narrow slit cut into a glass window.

Croatian lines are but symbols of the country's discriminatory (and often dysfunctional) system. On either side of the glass partition it is US and THEM. Them who have the power, the information, access. Them, the nurses, the bureaucrats, the ticket sellers. The queue is like the thread of life and we line up before the Fates, waiting to see if we get to see the doctor, if we have all of our paperwork in order for our visa, ID, or parking permit. Or we line up just to ask where we can find the other line. Do you want something in Croatia? Yes? THEN GET IN LINE!!!

Believe it or not, but this is not how it is in the U.S. Now, I thought I understood lines when living in America, but after befriending several people from former-Communist countries I was informed that we, Americans, know nothing of lines. We do have lines in the U.S., but they are temporary affairs. Like a spring shower, not a storm.

You know how when you go to McDonald's and if you stand in line for a few seconds someone will hop onto the next register and ask if they can help you? Well, it's pretty much like that EVERYWHERE in America. There are no glass partitions in the doctor's office. There are no doors that are impossible to open from the outside. Service, anywhere, is quick. If it's not, then you get to complain. You get to remember people's names, talk to managers and supervisors. You hear apologies and assurances that it won't happen again. Even if you are stuck in line, you still feel empowered.

In Croatia, nothing drains your sense of agency faster than standing in line. Anything you have done in your life, the very things that give you some sense of self-worth have been stripped away, leaving nothing but the bare bones of a pathetic, insignificant existence. You're just another corpse in purgatory. Another number in the factory. And just when you start to take some solace in the fact that before the line we are all equal, you see one of the chosen float to the front. You see an individual bathed in the divine light of favor, progressing ahead of everyone else. This angelic spirit has been gifted with the wings of *veze*, a heavenly connection gifted by her devotion to the gods. She sails forward. And you wait with the rest of the bums.

At this point the line descends into chaos. It morphs from a row of people waiting into a clump of animals herding, trying to get closer and closer to its end. Maneuvering through this huddle requires artistry. Years of practice seem to pay off. The older ladies are able to call the nurse by name, asking about her relations, holiday or some other personal detail lost to the rest of us. These pleasantries are like a verbal foot in the door, enabling the interlocutor to then plead to be taken ahead of her turn. For those of us lacking in the conversational talents we at least have one gift, elbows. Amid the herd we stick our arms out akimbo blocking the frail and advantage-seeking senior citizens. We push and jostle until finally we press against the partition or threshold, and then like everyone else we plead our case, hoping for admittance.

I'm not sure why there is such a difference between the service one receives in the U.S. and what we get in Croatia. It might be a scarcity of resources. Employers often keep the number of on-duty employees to a minimum. Or it might be a difference in protocol. When I worked in a large chain of bookstores, lines were as hated by management as they were by the customers. If more than four people queued before the register we called for backup, just like the police. Then everyone everywhere stopped what they were doing and came to expedite customers through the line. During the holiday rush we gave out free coffee and samples of food from the in-store Starbucks. In terms of state institutions you would think that in a country with 200,000 civil servants, who are largely paid with the taxed 47% of our income and the 25% sales tax on everything, there would be more than enough people available to speed up our wait time. Then again, perhaps the long lines endure, just like the glass partitions, in order to preserve that power imbalance between those who makes us wait, and those of us who are waiting.

CHAPTER 28

ZET

In Tulsa we have the idea of public transport. There are buses, but by a practical measure they just serve as an image of a bigger idea. Functionally, they hardly exist at all. The buses come by each stop once every hour, stop running at 5 p.m. and don't really take you anywhere all that useful. One of the few times I actually rode a bus was in preschool as a class, and I think that was just so we would know what a bus was. We also went to the downtown library, so we could know what a downtown library was, or that we had one.

Public transit in Zagreb is fantastic, the trains are new, clean, and well-maintained. They run frequently and travel extensively throughout the city. Unlike in Tulsa where you can live most of your life without engaging in public transit, the tramway in Zagreb is an integral part of life.

And this makes the reality of the tramway all the more ironic: Zagreb has a great tram system, and yet most people ride it for free. Riding the tram depends mostly on the honor system. There is no fee for entering the tram, no turnstile, gate, nothing. You just hop on; however, you are supposed to buy a ticket in advance at a nearby kiosk or from the driver. There is some level of enforcement. Uniformed inspectors come around from time to time and check your tickets. If you cannot show them one you are fined 200 *kuna* (roughly $40).

Part of the lore of Zagreb are all the stories about how people have attempted to get of out paying the fine. One of the more clever ones I've heard involved a friend who had already been riding on the tram when an inspector (called *kontrolor* in Croatian) entered. Once the tram started moving he ran up to her, pretending to be nervous and asked her if he still had time to purchase his ticket on his phone (this was when you could use your phone to buy a ticket, a process since suspended under confusing circumstances). The inspector, a little shocked at being directly approached, replied in a relaxing tone that of course there was still time.

When you're caught, inspectors exit the tram with you and write you a ticket on the side of the street. Another friend, an American married to a Croatian, related to me how once when he was caught he played dumb, acting like he didn't speak Croatian, was only here for a conference, and couldn't understand this "crazy" tram system. As he was on the cusp of success, having almost convinced the inspectors he was just a dumb tourist when a tram full of his former students stopped and they all yelled: "Hi Dave!" He ended up paying the fine. I've heard from other foreigners that they too act as foreign as possible. According to these stories the inspectors will get so frustrated trying to get you to understand them that they will eventually just let you go.

Usually, you just try to dodge the inspectors. When they enter, you exit. They are pretty easy to spot. They wear blue jackets with stripped blue button-down shirts, and have a way of parting the most densely packed crowds like Moses parted the Red Sea.

Another preoccupation among free riders is trying to anticipate the inspectors' behavior. It is assumed that inspectors don't work after 8 or 9 p.m. or early on weekends, some assume they don't work weekends at all. I've also been told that inspectors won't work when its raining, snowy, or frigidly cold. I'm not sure if it is assumed that inspectors don't want to stand in the rain, snow or cold when writing a ticket or if would it would be socially unacceptable to make a passenger stand in bad weather when getting a fine. In any case it assumed that fines for free riding are canceled due to inclement weather. I'm not sure if any of this is true.

The free riding is just a logical part of living in Zagreb. Illegal, but logical, welcome to Croatia. The economists tell us that few will pay for something if they can obtain it for free. Given the paltry system of enforcement it's rational that few people pay for a tram ride. Since the fine is 200 *kuna* and a tram ride itself costs 10 *kuna*, if you can ride for free 20 or more times without paying, then it's worth risking the fine. The times I do buy a ticket are when I'm either riding with my daughter or mother-in-law. And these are social inducements. I don't want people to think that I'm a bad father when they see me holding my little girl and getting fined by the inspectors on the side of the street. (Also, since she speaks Croatian she would blow my cover as a dumb tourist.) My other friends have related similar reasons. One woman told me that since she was now over 35 (and on TV) she would be embarrassed if she was seen being fined.

But there is also another economic argument and this returns to the discrepancy between policy and practice. A tram ride costs 10 *kuna*, which is about $2. Now imagine if you had to ride the tram twice a day to get to work and back. That would be $4 a day, $20 a week, $80 a month, $960 a year. In a country where the average monthly salary is between $800 and $1,000 a month, that's nearly 10% or more of your annual income, just to get to work. What's more is that ZET (the tram operator) knows that most people do not or cannot pay this fare. Danas.hr reported that while 298 million people rode the tram (and buses) last year, revenue was only at 319 million *kuna*! That's less than 1.5 *kuna* per person, roughly $0.25 a passenger.

Last year, they raised the price from 10 to 15 *kuna*, and since then revenue stayed roughly the same. ZET was now earning less than it was before if you consider the price increase. It was as if Joseph Heller and Franz Kafka jointly designed this policy. *ZET raises the price to make less money!!* The politicians know no one is paying the price, the passengers know it, ZET knows it, and yet the price that no one pays endured. Finally, they lowered it again. I don't know whether or not this has resulted in generating more revenue.

This is how life is here. In Croatia, we exist in a world where policy after policy, law after law attempt to impose an impossible standard on our reality. As a result, our daily life is learning how to dodge the rules, and to define the actual distance between the imaginary and the real, to discern the actual difference between what is demanded and what is permissible. For all that, Croatia pays a greater price; a fare-less ride on the tram only sounds free.

CHAPTER 29

Zablogreb

Life is funny. Just when you're set for one destination, the winds of fate come and take you somewhere else completely different. I wanted to be a former house painter/English teacher in Oklahoma. Now I live in Croatia. Just when you think things are at their worst, being fired from a bookstore or ending up career-less in Croatia, things can suddenly turn around. The glass seems half-full, but that's fortunate because it's filled with poison. Life is full of zigzags and switchbacks, each direction hinges more on ill-conceived acts of heart than on the things we mull over and plan down to the finest detail. It's like I had been sailing to boring ol' Philadelphia, fell in love, leapt with my heart and ended up in *fucking* Zanzibar.

After my fruitless search for employment, I eventually found a job teaching a few English classes at a private institute in the evening. The pay was low. This was reality: after a bachelor's degree, a master's, and a Ph.D., I was making the same amount of money I made when I was 16 and working at a grocery store.

Ah, Croatia. Really though, I was just happy to have a job, a reason to leave the house. Bored with the text books, I tried to get my students to talk about things that interested them. In one class we talked mostly about the EU and Economics. I was becoming acquainted with regular Croatians and started understanding Croatia a bit better.

At the end of November, I had an idea to start a blog about the economics and politics in Croatia. I called it *Zablogreb* because *Zagreb Blog* was already taken and it sounded ridiculous. I really thought that this would just be a way for me to help understand what I understood about Croatia, and help explain Croatia to my American friends and family. After a few posts about tax reform and Croatia's fiscal policies, a friend gave me some good advice:

"Quit writing about boring stuff!" she said. Hmm…good idea. I decided to write something funny about culture. So, I did. Basically about our neighbor Paula and how in Croatia friends can say "Fuck your mother!" to each other and to your one-year-old daughter, but friends can never, ever, say "no" to each other! Then I tried to be funny again, and again. And finally I wrote a post about *Drinking Coffee in Croatia*, chapter 4 of this book, and that changed my life.

The post went viral. Suddenly, my posts were getting tens of tweets and thousands of Facebook likes. The blog went from getting 1,156 page views in December to receiving 110,098 in

January. Something was happening. I started getting messages from Croats in America thanking me for explaining what they had been trying or wanting to explain to their friends and in-laws for weeks, months or possibly years. I got messages from the spouses of Croatians saying they completely understood what I was writing about. One girl even sent me a message telling me her mom and grandma both sent her a link to my blog on the same day. We had three generations of readers! And then in February, it happened, the pinnacle of any blogger's career. We were NUMBER ONE on GOOGLE! If you Googled *propuh*, *Zablogreb* was in first place! Yes!

I started getting introduced by friends as "the guy that writes *Zablogreb*" with an "Oh" of recognition in their eyes. My wife's friends told her how much they liked it. One even referred to me as a friend when someone else mentioned the blog. **THIS IS MAKING IT IN CROATIA:** when people you've met once, want to refer to you as a friend. At one point I was hospitalized and both of the patients sharing the room with me, had read *Zablogreb*. I was on a airplane and both people beside me, had also read *Zablogreb*.

Then in mid-February of that year, I got asked to teach English at the Department of Political Science. It wasn't the ever elusive "steady employment," but I was teaching at the University. Around the same time the media began taking notice of me. In a few short months I was featured in all of Croatia's major newspapers and on the main television channels. In September, I got a book contract for the book you are currently holding in your hands (or reading illegally from the internet). About a year after I started *Zablogreb*, I was writing a blog for Croatia Radio Television, giving talks around the country based on the blog for one of the country's biggest publishers, and daring to call myself a writer.

All because I decided to start a silly blog about my mother-in-law, her neighbors, and Croatian culture. Who could have ever planned any of that? And the best thing about the success of *Zablogreb* is that it has helped me integrate into Croatian society. Recalling those early days and months when I felt like nothing but a foreigner, a complete stranger, I now, no longer feel foreign at all. I'm a like: *Outta da way, bona fide hrvatski zet coming through!*

The acceptance and support I have received from the readers has been incredible. The blog literally has thousands of comments, most of them supportive. For a country, a people who are generally skeptical of…well…everything, the way readers have embraced and encouraged *Zablogreb* has been most incredible. What's more is that all my luck and good fortune have come without the use of *veze*. We never asked for a favor or called in some social debt. That above all, makes me optimistic.

So, is this the happy ending? I hope not. I hope it's just the beginning. We still don't know what we are doing, but who ever does?

CHAPTER 30

Giving My Daughter the American Dream?

I no longer like going home. It's a strange experience that happens to the best of us living abroad. As you adapt to one culture, you turn around and see that you have, ever so slowly, disoriented yourself from your own (except for walking around barefoot and standing in the *propuh,* I still do that). And when you live abroad, you forget that time doesn't stop with your absence. It keeps marching on while your version of home is constructed, not by the world you encounter daily, but instead it is built by the residue of nostalgia. No longer made up of the physical facts on the ground, but by the emotions and impressions of memory. You can never go home, because that home no longer exists, except in your heart and head. As the tangible world moves further away from the one that exists in yourself, so too does the inner yearning for what was once past increase.

In Croatia I keep thinking about the phone we had hanging in our kitchen when I was growing up. It was "the" phone and so it had to have a long iconic cord attached to it, one that could stretch through just about most of the downstairs. Imagine, today, encountering a beige, curly, rubber cord vibrating in the spaces between doors, crisscrossing and wrapping around corners? Impossible. Yet, once I think about this phone cord, I then think about the size of our house, having my own room, stairs, a backyard, a front yard, a driveway, then the whole neighborhood forms, the houses, trees and fences fall into place. The whole of American society can be constructed from my thoughts about a *fucking* phone cord. This, I believe, is the definition of longing. Like when you see something seemingly insignificant left over from a horribly ended relationship, an old lighter, an empty pack of cigarettes, and you can relive the whole experience all over again. Marcel Proust had some cookies. I have a phone cord.

Remembering is a strange affair because I simultaneously want to go home, but also understand that there is no longer any home to go to. Everything is more complicated when Sara as an entity, a being, a person, is factored into this awkward equation of self, place, memory, identity and the future. What do I want for her? I want what I had, but does that mean I want us to live in America? Or just the bygone America of my youth? How do you know what to give your child when you're in a new place, a place that has nothing to offer from the life you were given? Can I give her the American Dream in Croatia?

Part of being a parent is reliving your childhood through the different stages of your own kid's development. But as a parent here there is nothing for me to relive. No, I didn't go to the seaside as a kid, and we never went to the main square just because (in Oklahoma we don't even have a sea or main square). My sister has two kids and lives in a nice area of Washington, D.C. She is living the closest thing to the American Dream. She and her husband have a house. We rent an apartment. Her kids have bedrooms, a backyard, summers of air-conditioning, carpool and Target. Sara has a bed, a park, and German-named stores. My niece and nephew's childhood will be reminiscent of what my sister and I had. It may be even better. All I know for certain is that here, in Croatia, Sara's life will be different. Part of me desperately wants her to know what an American childhood is like. Like the father who, failed to be the star football player, exerts pressure on his own son to be what he wasn't, I worry that I will try to make Sara too American. *We will go barefoot to McDonald's every day and eat in front of a fan!*

This is the immigrant's dilemma. Now I know what my Irish and German ancestors must have thought as they saw their children and grandchildren shed the habits and culture of the old country. I want to be here, but I also want Sara to be an American. Which sounds stupid, really. Why do I want her to be an American, when she's lived in Croatia her whole life?

Nevertheless, I am raising my daughter in this strange place filled with the odd customs like party breaking, gift giving, *propuh, papuče, veze*, black BMWs, and dudes in tracksuits with fanny packs. So, what I've been trying to do is to embrace all of the different things that inform Sara's upbringing: Split neighbors, lunchtime, her overbearing grandma, parks, and trips to the seaside. In my most uncertain moments, when doubt is at its highest, I just listen to what my sister said: "Dude, don't worry about it. You. Live. In. Europe. And we all wish we lived in Europe."

Never mind the fact that Europe probably looks something from a Jean Luc-Godard film, *Casablanca*, or the *Bourne Identity*. And in reality, my life is more like a Woody Allen film with less romance and comedy, just the frustration and anxiety. But hey, at least it's like a movie, and maybe that and that alone is the American Dream.

EPILOGUE

Punica Goes to America

The plane landed in Chicago and as we were taxiing to the gate, Vida looked out the window, noticing the crunchy grass, dried and dead in the hot Illinois sun.

"Croatia is prettier." She exclaimed. I pointed out that we were still on the tarmac of O'Hare Airport. Two minutes on the ground and her opinion was already set. America: kind of disappointing.

I, on the other hand, was ecstatic to be home, and this time with my entire family. I was convinced that the hardest thing would be coming back to Croatia. What more could I want, America plus Vana and Sara, even *punica*! A match made in heaven…crr…almost.

My youngest sister was getting married that summer, so the family had helped pay for the four of us to fly home. Only my mom and stepfather had met any of our Croatian in-laws. So, Vida was here as an ambassador from one family to the next.

What she expected or thought America would be like was beyond me. When I came to Croatia I had hardly ever heard of Croatia. Sure, I knew there had been a war and it was once communist. The end. But, for someone like Vida, America had always been a bit of a mystery. Something that everyone knew about (and had an opinion about), but also a place that was unknown. Then she got an American for a son-in-law, which I think just heightened her curiosity. Before leaving she asked me:

"When we get to America, will there be cafes like there are here?" I wanted to laugh. I looked at Vida with wide-eyed amusement and explained that on our street in Vrbik, there are around nine cafes. Not only is this not normal for America, it's not normal for the rest of the world. I regrettably informed her that I wasn't even sure if there were nine cafes in Tulsa, let alone any near my mother's house. Welcome to culture shock.

Of course in any of the cafes in Oklahoma, you can't smoke. And the temperature for most of the trip was never under 95° F. Nothing says *mmm* like a hot cup of coffee outside in the sweltering Oklahoma heat with a cigarette soaking up the sweat from your fingers. Eventually, I took Vida to a Starbucks in a posh, open-air shopping center that's the closest you can get to "Europe" in all of Oklahoma. We sat outside, while she smoked and drank a latte. With a mix of bafflement and disgust she contemplated the giant paper cup and its plastic lid as if it were something extraterrestrial, or futuristic, perhaps it's what astronauts use to drink their coffee in space. What was more bewildering were the 12 liquid ounces inside. I could see it on her face, the same exact question I had asked during my first visit to Split: *Where the hell is the coffee?*

But we had other issues too. Sara was sick. She came down with a fever the day after we arrived and had some um… bathroom issues (you're welcome teenage future Sara). On the fifth day we took her to the emergency room. Fortunately we had travel insurance because a four-hour stay in the ER cost $1,300.00!!! Silly me, I had grown accustomed to taking my daughter to the doctor whenever she was sick, for free.

In Vrbik we lived within walking distance of a grocery store, and by "walking distance" I mean 30 seconds from our apartment's entrance. In Oklahoma the nearest grocery store was about a mile and a half away. I drove, but since I was used to going to the grocery store just whenever I needed to go to the grocery store, I'd forgotten how to buy in bulk. I would park, traverse the store's vast asphalt plains, enter, and buy what was immediately on my mind, often something for Sara, and then I would leave only to get home and have someone say: "Did you remember to get *blah blah blah?*" A perfectly reasonable request that I completely forgot about. So then, I would back the car out of the driveway, turn onto the street, drive here, turn there, turn again, drive some more, park, finish listening to a news story on the radio and then go shopping. It was exhausting.

Our trip consolidated how accustomed I had become to life in Croatia. It wasn't that I had accepted certain aspects of the culture, it was that I now preferred them. Of course without the experience of returning home, I would have never believed that this was the case. I would have still imagined that living in Croatia was a compromise, not something that I wanted for myself, but something I was doing for Vana and Sara. Only now could I understand that leaving Oklahoma and America was my choice. Before, I believed that my longing for Croatia was really just a longing for Vana; however, now with her and Sara here, I still didn't feel at home. Our life was in Zagreb. I understood that now.

Seeing the U.S. through Vida's experience amplified the new strangeness with which I encountered everything. At one point I found Vida looking longingly out of the first-floor window, which she couldn't open because it would let all the cold air out and the 101° F air in. She looked to me and said, with a hint of strange sadness in her voice that no one was outside. It was true. Amid the manicured lawns and driveways there wasn't a soul to be seen. It was another glimpse of how lonely and isolating America can be. By this time in Croatia, I would have met most of the neighbors. We hadn't met a single one. I didn't even know any of my mother's neighbors' names.

Other *punica* observations were more amusing than sad. With some of her comments I felt a vindication, like *Aha! See that's how I felt in Split!* She pointed out to me that no one seemed to be in a constant state of planning and preparing lunch. *Duh.* I explained that no one was planning lunch because "we" are actually not that concerned about lunch. We do not live in a state of fear that not knowing what you are going to eat is almost the same as starving. In Croatia, Vida would ask me what I wanted for lunch tomorrow while I was still eating the day's lunch. In Tulsa, no one organized their day around lunch. When dinner came around my mom either looked to see what she had in her giant freezer or refrigerator, or we ordered Chinese food. Also, we were busy making the rounds at various family functions.

Now, of course in Croatia when you go to someone's house for lunch or dinner, you are always, ALWAYS, asked if you want more, and no matter what you say, no matter how much you refuse, say no, or no thanks, you will always get more. There will be more! And it will be on your plate!

In the U.S., the host will just ask once, and believe you when you say that you don't want anymore. Why would you lie?

"Would you like some more?"

"No thanks."

"OK."

Before arriving in the U.S., and a few more times when we were there, I warned Vida about this. I told her, "Just say yes if you want more and no if you *really* don't." It doesn't sound that complicated, does it? It is. She just couldn't do it. Years of Croatian upbringing, millions of meals hosted and a few thousand of her being hosted had left their indelible mark on her manners: she could never say "yes" on the first question. And so, she was always hungry. When I wasn't distracted with Sara or seeing the rest of my family, I would remember to sneak over to Vida as the plates were being cleared and ask her if she wasn't *really* still hungry and if she was sure she didn't *really* want more. Even then, I'm not sure if her refusals for seconds were genuine.

Then there were the horrors of American parenting. My sister and her two kids were also staying with my mom (and for the record I think my sister is a great parent). It was a test to all of Vida's Croatian grandmotherly instincts. My four-year-old niece and one-year-old nephew traipsed around the house barefoot. In the air-conditioning! Granted it was 100° F and over outside, but inside it was a cool 72° F. What's worse, they didn't even own a pair of slippers because you know, they're not Disney characters. Outside, at a family BBQ, they ran around barefoot. And on one Saturday when my sister arranged for the cousins to have their pictures taken in a nice park, my niece began running through the sprinklers. Soaking wet clothes, wet hair and barefoot she road back to the house in the air-conditioned car. I imagine it was like Peter Parker having to ignore his own Spider Sense. *Baka (Grandma) sense tingling!*

And yet American convention prevented her from saving anyone. Vida also couldn't believe how my nephew was left to eat on his own. Sat in his high chair he was given food and fed himself, at one year old! In Croatia, mothers and grandmothers frequently feed their kids until they are about…oh…32.

The one thing Vida did enjoy, which is what every Croatian who travels to America also takes delight in, cheap stuff! Vida and my mother would go on shopping trips and Vida would come back with pillow cases, duvet covers, or towels and show it to me in a state of pride and disbelief. She became a master of division and multiplication, establishing the exchange rate.

"This was only 30 *kunas*. Isn't it beautiful? 30 *kunas*! I can't believe it." Of course most of what she bought went to other people as gifts.

Well, after two weeks we came back to Croatia. It was an arduous journey complete with canceled flights, a jet-lagged two-year-old, and an exhausted *punica*. We left on Saturday morning and arrived in our apartment in Zagreb at 11:30 p.m. on Monday! This trip though was an important milestone for me. I had dreamed about being back home with Vana, Sara, and Vida, believing that if I had my family with me, I would love the U.S. as much as I did when I was a kid. Nope. From the vast distances surrounding everything, to the empty streets, to the common concern over street crime, the life I had become accustomed to in Croatia was now too different from life in America. I could no longer move seamlessly between these two worlds. I would have to pick one and hope for the best.

When we arrived in Zagreb, I had to drive Vida and our luggage to the apartment and then return to the bus station for Vana and Sara (we took a bus from the airport). It was near midnight and I left my wife and sleeping daughter outside of the bus station. This would never, ever, happen in the U.S., anywhere! Last time I was at the bus station in Tulsa, I was offered some crack cocaine and another guy was stabbed. But, in Zagreb, well in Zagreb or anywhere in Croatia, you can leave your wife and daughter unmolested at midnight outside of the bus station. This is me screaming: *See! See, how different it is!?!*

The next day I took Sara to the park. I held her hand while also carrying her tricycle. We walked down the footpath named after the cosmonaut Yuri Gagarin. The pavement was shaded, dappled by the sunlight breaking through the leaves above. People walked around us. A dog bounded in the grass. A few groups of friends happily conversed under the umbrellas of a nearby cafe. In the near distance the number 4 tram rattled down Savska street. And I was filled with a serene calm. I put Sara's trike down, she climbed on and began riding away. She laughed, cruising over the bumps in fissure-like cracks as fast as she could. It took me a second to understand what was happening. Then I got it. Sara raced farther and farther away. I started running after her, knowing now, more than ever, that I was happy to be home.

ACKNOWLEDGMENTS

I would like to express my gratitude to the many people and things that helped make this story possible. First, to my friends and colleagues at the Faculty of Political Sciences at the University of Zagreb and Glas Hrvatske, the University of Kansas Center for Russian and Eastern European Studies, and the U.S. Department of State's Fulbright Program.

Though I have received an immeasurable amount of support from many people there are a few I am greatly indebted to: Ivana Pavlović who invited me to give the talk that started this whole business, Mija Pavliša whose early optimism was greatly needed, Helena Puljiz, Mate Šubašić, Jelena Primorac, Mijo Bebić, Danko Cenić Ivana Jukić, Alex Simmons, my editors Dana Früschütz and Ana Briški Durdevac, my publisher Neven Antičević, the neighbors in Split, family, both Croatian and American, my dear *punica*, all four of my incredible parents, my inspiring siblings, everyone who ever read, liked, shared or commented on *Zablogreb*, and most of all my biggest critic, greatest fan, frequent translator and wonderful wife, Silvana, who really is the reason for all of it.

ABOUT THE AUTHOR

Cody McClain Brown teaches at the University of Zagreb and writes a weekly blog for Croatian Radio Television's the *Voice of Croatia*. He has a Ph.D. in political science and lives in Zagreb with his wife and daughter—his mother-in-law visits frequently.